WOODSLANE WALKING GUIDES

The GREAT OCEAN WALK

by

Julie Mundy & Debra Heyes

WOODSLANE PRESS

Woodslane Press Pty Ltd
10 Apollo Street
Warriewood NSW 2102
Australia
Email: info@woodslane.com.au
Tel: (02) 8445 2300 woodslanepress.com.au

First published in Australia in 2022 by Woodslane Press, reprinted 2025

NATIONAL LIBRARY OF AUSTRALIA

A catalogue record for this book is available from the National Library of Australia

FSC
www.fsc.org
MIX
Supporting responsible forestry
FSC® C151165

Printed in China by Jilin GIGO
Designed by Jenny Cowan
Cover image: Debra Heyes

The GREAT OCEAN WALK

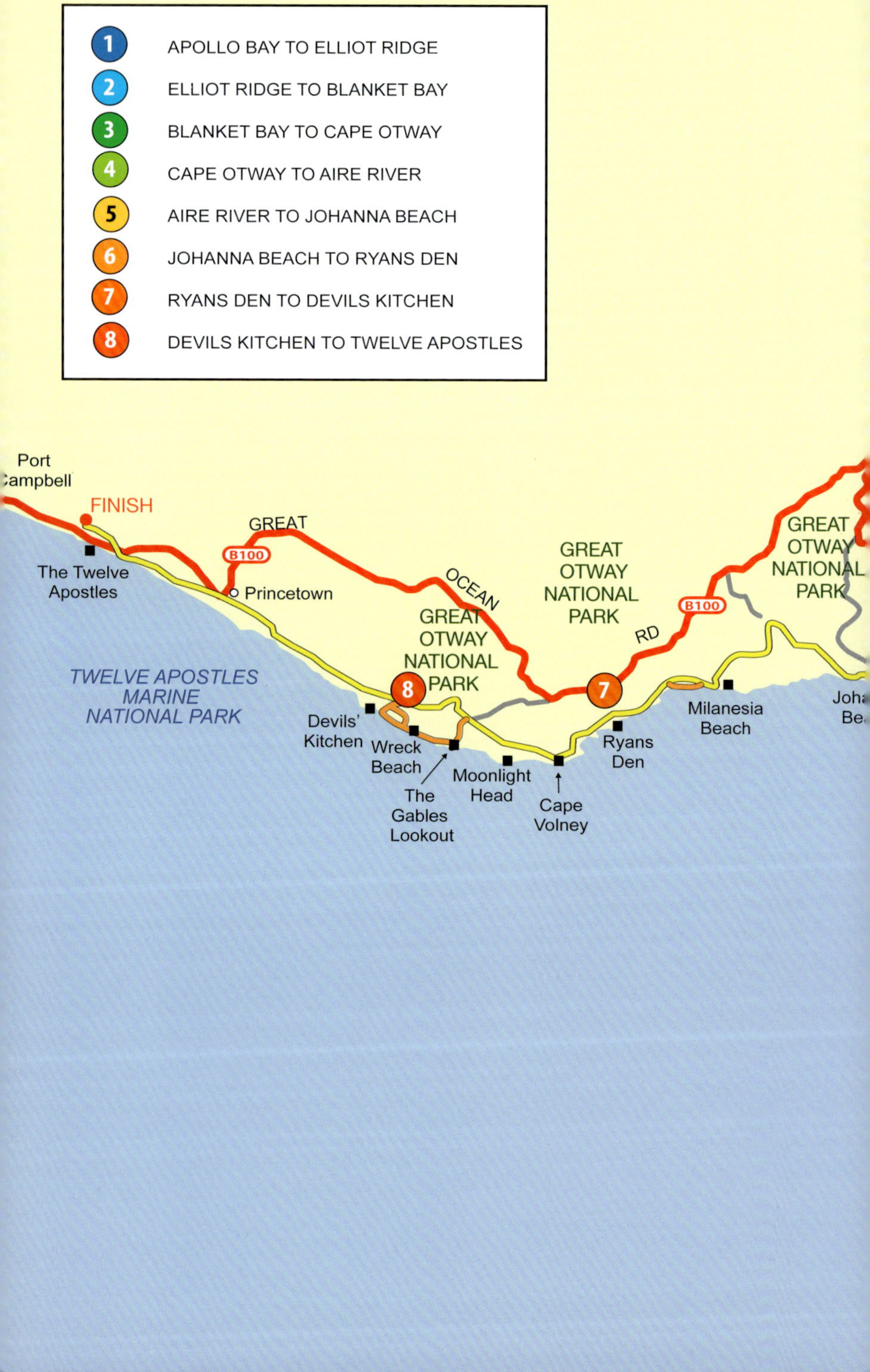
1 APOLLO BAY TO ELLIOT RIDGE
2 ELLIOT RIDGE TO BLANKET BAY
3 BLANKET BAY TO CAPE OTWAY
4 CAPE OTWAY TO AIRE RIVER
5 AIRE RIVER TO JOHANNA BEACH
6 JOHANNA BEACH TO RYANS DEN
7 RYANS DEN TO DEVILS KITCHEN
8 DEVILS KITCHEN TO TWELVE APOSTLES
Port
FINISH
The Twelve Apostles
GREAT OCEAN RD
B100
Princetown
GREAT OTWAY NATIONAL PARK
GREAT OTWAY NATIONAL PARK
GREAT OTWAY NATIONAL PARK
B100
TWELVE APOSTLES MARINE NATIONAL PARK
8
7
Devils' Kitchen
Wreck Beach
The Gables Lookout
Moonlight Head
Cape Volney
Ryans Den
Milanesia Beach

Walk Location

Contents

Overview map ...... **iv-v**

Introduction and preparation **1**

Itinerary options **23**

The Great Ocean Walk

Day 1 29

Day 2 41

Day 3 49

Day 4 61

Day 5 69

Day 6 77

Day 7 87

Day 8 95

Safety tips **106**

Regional Wildlife **114**

Regional Birdlife **116**

Regional Flora **120**

Regional Fungi **122**

Useful Contacts **124**

Further Reading **132**

Index **134**

About the authors and acknowledgements **136**

Photography credits **137**

Other books from Woodslane Press **140**

Map symbols and legend **142**

Cape Otway Lightstation Point Franklin

Introduction and preparation

The 100-kilometre Great Ocean Walk (GOW) is rightly considered one of Australia's iconic multi-day walks. Highly doable by almost all experience levels, it is an easily accessed and flexible walk along Victoria's wild and stunning southern coast. It accommodates options for day walkers, through-walkers, and self-supporting end-to-end campers. Be prepared for roaring seas, soaring sea cliffs, rolling sand dunes, lighthouses, shipwrecks, river crossings, wild sandy beaches and lush fern gullies. At the end is the breathtaking approach to the world-famous Twelve Apostles. The entire GOW is designed to be walked east to west (this is a requirement for those camping), though you will occasionally come across walkers coming the opposite way doing one of the circuits or sidetracks. But generally, this approach means that the track rarely feels overcrowded, despite there not being a booking system which limits daily walkers (though the camp sites do have strict limits which means you need to book early). The 8-day 'standard' itinerary is entirely achievable by most reasonably fit people, who don't mind some ups and downs. As with all hiking, putting in some regular training in advance of the walk, especially if you are carrying a full pack, will ensure a much more enjoyable experience.

The GOW is generally very well signposted (thank you, Parks Victoria!), with fairly regular distance markers and regular GOW 'flash' marks so you can check you are on track — very helpful when you come to intersections, so keep an eye out for them. The track is maintained at least twice a year (usually in March and November), so generally the path is easy to follow, although there are exceptions. This guidebook will provide some additional information on waypoints and on some of the alternate routes; it will help you plan the walk that suits you best and enhance your experience along the way, with additional information on local history, sights, flora and fauna.

Introduction

Traditional Owners: the Eastern Maar (Gadubanud and Girrai Wurrung)

The Traditional Owners of the land which is traversed by the Great Ocean Walk, and of the surrounding Otway region covered in this book, are the lands of the Gadubanud (meaning 'King Parrot people') or Yarro waetch, and Girrai Wurrung people, today drawn together as the Eastern Maar. Their Country covers most of south-western Victoria and extends from Ararat in the north, west to Warnambool and Port Fairy, and east along the Great Ocean Road as far as Aireys Inlet. Eastern Maar Country responsibilities extend some 100 metres into the sea and so also includes the Twelve Apostles. The Eastern Maar have been present in this area for some 35,000 years and their responsibility to care for Country and culture continues uninterrupted. There is only limited documented knowledge of the Gadubanud peoples, who successfully avoided European colonisers until the 1830s but then experienced an intensely difficult and tragic period of decimation through to the 1880s due to horrific massacres and the catastrophic impact of introduced diseases.

We do know that the Gadubanud used bark canoes in the waters of the coast and river estuaries. On some days of the GOW, you may come across some of the many coastal shell 'middens' of the Gadubanud, who enjoyed a rich and diverse diet of shellfish, eels, Cape Barren geese, seals, ducks, berries and tubers. If you do come across a midden, please avoid disturbing these important cultural heritage sites by not walking on them or removing anything from them. Middens are typically in sandy soils, near to the coast and estuaries, and are identified by an unusually high concentration of old whitened shells and other food debris in a roughly defined area, sometimes in a large mound or heap.

Today the Eastern Maar have a continuing responsibility for Country which provides them with sanctuary and physical and spiritual sustenance. They are actively involved in the governance and planning of the use of the Great Ocean Walk and surrounding National Parks, and in the new Great Ocean Road Parks and Coast Authority. We wish to acknowledge their ongoing connection with and care for the land and sea, their culture and language, and we pay our respects to their leaders, past, present and emerging. We also acknowledge other First Nations people who may be walking the GOW. We wish to advise First Nations people that there is some further information provided on the

Blanket Bay massacre, in an effort to educate and inform, on page 67 of the Guidebook which you may find distressing. We ask that GOW walkers also pay respect to and honour the Traditional Custodians and the land on which you walk — perhaps through endeavouring to learn and understand more of this rich and important heritage, and certainly by treading lightly on your walks. Part of this respect is not removing anything from the walks, including rocks, shells and flora — please ensure photographs and treasured memories are your only souvenirs.

When to walk

The GOW offers wonderful and quite varied walking at different times of the year. Many people come back to experience it in all its seasons. Being on the edge of the Southern Ocean, and subject to weather coming from either side of Cape Otway, it is not unusual to experience all the seasons in one single day. Wind is quite a constant, blowing up off the oceans, and it can rain at any time, so be well prepared with waterproof and warm clothing, even in summer. Annual rainfall can reach 1200-1800 mm, making it one of the wettest parts of Victoria. Rolling sea fogs can make some of the walking through the forests mysterious and atmospheric. If you ask 10 people who have hiked the GOW about the weather, you will hear 10 different stories!

In summer, and on all very hot days (which can reach 30°C), you need to be very conscious of managing heat (some of the sections are exposed and heat stress is a concern), water access and intake, sunburn

Introduction

protection and keeping a close eye out for snakes. It is wise to begin very early on these days and finish before the heat of the day. You will also need to monitor the bushfire danger rating each day as parks may close with little notice (see page 21 on bushfire safety).

Autumn often provides (but not always!) the most stable weather, with cooler nights and more moderate daytime temperatures. Winter means being prepared for shorter days as it gets dark by 5pm during May-August. Windy, wet and spectacular weather is the norm. This can range from short showers to an all-day drenching, which can be challenging for campers trying to dry their tents each day. With wet weather comes the joy (!) of leeches along some of the wetter sections — but a lesser concern for snakes (though even on colder sunny days they may be out basking on the path in the sun). Autumn and winter are the best time of year for fungi lovers and the GOW has some wonderful offerings. You are also much more likely to have the walk to yourself, so if you are hardy and dress accordingly, it can be a wonderful time to walk.

Spring is the most changeable time of year, weather-wise, and sudden showers and squalls are not uncommon, along with sometimes beautiful sunny days and crisp nights, but this is when the wildflowers come into their own: you have the opportunity to spot some of Victoria's rare native orchids and many other types of flowering plants. Snakes and lizards also start to re-emerge to warm in the sun patches in the centre of the paths.

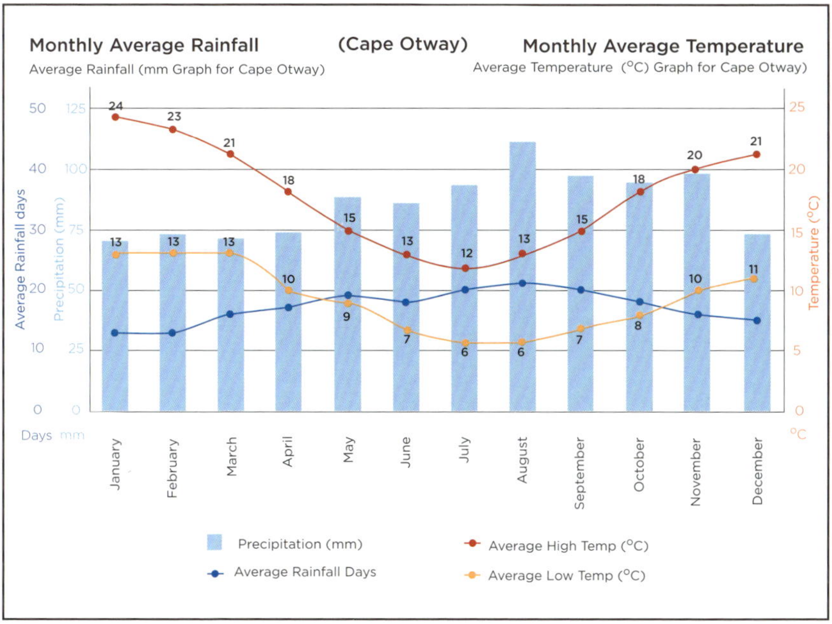

How to use this book

The GOW is officially (the Parks Victoria recommendation) split up into eight 'walk days'. There are slightly different start/finishes and distances indicated for those who are camping and for those who are day-walking (linked to transport access/exit points). We have also included itinerary options (4, 5, 6, 8, 9 days), and a 'Build Your Own Walk', showing distances between access points (pages 24-25) for those wanting to tailor their walk further. If you are walking with a tour company (guided or independently) they will also be able to tailor itineraries to suit your situation and requirements.

Each day section describes key waypoints, but we recommend you also keep an eye out for the GOW flashes/marks. This guide aims to provide additional information and points of interest along the way. We recommend you also purchase the *Great Ocean Walk Information Guide and Official Map* to accompany this guidebook, though the maps contained herein will be sufficient if you are following the standard 8-day route.

On each day we have also included a table with a description of the various options/decision points along the route — these generally

Introduction

involve a choice between inland (recommended by Parks Victoria) and low tide beach options. As with Parks Victoria, our recommendation is that you take the official inland routes where they are available, unless otherwise indicated. These southern coastlines are wild, remote and can be unpredictable. Only attempt beach options at low or outgoing tides and be conscious that they sometimes involve traversing deep rock gutters and scrambling. Some of the options have no intermediate exit/escape points, with tall sea cliffs, so err on the side of caution.

At the back of the book you will find contact details for accommodation options (by area/region), guided walk operators, transport providers and further information on flora and fauna you might encounter along the way.

Walk grades and times

Each of the days includes an indication of its grade and the time required to complete it. These are all generous estimates, working on about 3 km/hour to account for the hills, river crossings and beach-walking - allow longer if you prefer to take your time and enjoy the scenery or longer lunches in the sun. The grading is based on the most difficult sections of each day's walk.

Easy – mostly flat or minimal ascent/descent and suitable for all ages. May include short sections of steps or some easy/short beach walking.

Moderate – may contain steeper sections, with loose, rough or sandy ground and/or lots of steps and longer or sloping soft sand sections. Sturdy shoes recommended.

Hard – contains extended steep or rough sections, rock scrambling and/or extended beach walking in soft or sloping sand. Requires reasonable levels of fitness. Sturdy footwear essential.

Walking with children

The Great Ocean Walk may be doable for walk-fit and active older children and for teenagers, though it is only recommended for those who have considerable hiking experience; the one-way and remote nature of the track on some days means there is not always an easy exit option. It is a varied walk, different on each day, with lots to interest walkers of all ages: rockpools and beaches (beware of waves and only swim at patrolled beaches), creeks, shipwrecks, wallabies and echidnas. Keep a very close eye on children near the coastal cliffs and steeper bush sections, as they are rarely fenced, and most particularly on the river crossings which should only be attempted at low tide on calm days, even by adults.

Accessibility

The GOW as a whole is unfortunately not wheelchair accessible, nor suited to those with limited mobility, as there are extensive sections of beach walking including through soft sand, steep and sometimes slippery clay descents and many steps.

Tides

The Great Ocean Walk is named as it is for a reason — it traces along the Southern Ocean coastline of Victoria from Apollo Bay, around Cape Otway, through to the Twelve Apostles, passing dozens of shipwrecks (some remnants can be seen) along the way.

Introduction

The ocean here is wild: there is nothing between Antarctica and these shores, and the weather and swells can often be wild and woolly. For a number of the river crossings, and some of the beach options, **you will need to plan your walk around times of low and outgoing tides**. Some of the river crossings can be dangerous on incoming tides with a good swell, and you will need to either wait until the tide recedes or opt for an alternate inland route where available. Don't underestimate the power and unpredictability of the waves down here, especially when combined with high tides: there is a good reason this area is referred to as 'The Shipwreck Coast'.

We recommend you use either the Bureau of Meteorology website (www.bom.org.au) or the even more precise Willy Weather (www.willyweather.com.au), making sure you set it to your closest point (Apollo Bay, Cape Otway, Princetown) for that day's walk (tide times can vary by more than 30 minutes along the walk). Check the tide times daily, as they change. At certain times of the year (Spring) and month (full moons), maximum tide heights can change dramatically, with 'King Tides' not being uncommon. If there is a storm front or big winds, the swell of the waves can exacerbate this. On other days the ocean may well be flat and you will wonder what all the fuss is about. Don't be deceived: this is one of the most dangerous coastlines in Australia.

Independent or guided walk?

There are endless options available for the GOW, which is part of its attraction, depending on your experience, confidence, time available and preference. The walk itself is straightforward enough for those choosing to do it independently, with a bit of careful planning (including reading this guidebook), and is well signposted. The end-to-end self-supporting camping option is the toughest (though doable for most providing you can carry the weight) and most affordable. Some independent walkers might choose to base themselves at non-GOW camping grounds, caravan parks, motels, lodges, and arrange their own (two-car) or commercial shuttle services to take them to and from the start/end of each walk. Others with less time or experience might choose to use some of the excellent local accommodation providers and tour operators to provide a fully organised trip, either self-guided or guided. The choice is yours and all options are good! Contact details for tour operators and accommodation are provided in the back of this guide.

Transport options

Due to its remote nature, while transportation options for the GOW are available, it does take a bit of planning. More detailed information is included in the back of this guide.

Public transport to start of walk at Apollo Bay

Take the train from Melbourne Southern Cross Station to Geelong (about an hour) then bus from the station to Apollo Bay (about 2h 45m). The entire journey takes between 4-5 hours depending on connections. You can easily leave Melbourne early in the morning and complete the first day's walking on the same day. If you were running late, you could even get the bus as far as Marengo and miss the first flat section of the walk beside the Great Ocean Road from Apollo Bay.

Public transport from end of walk to Melbourne

The Apollo Bay to Warrnambool Bus Service picks people up from the Twelve Apostles Kiosk at the end of the walk. From the Twelve Apostles, it's approximately 2.5 scenic hours further on the bus, via Loch Ard Gorge, Port Campbell, London Bridge, Peterborough and Bay of Islands to Warnambool, where you can connect with a train back to Melbourne which takes approximately 3.5 hours. Alternatively, from the Twelve Apostles, you can take the bus in the opposite direction, back to Apollo Bay and further onto Geelong, to take the train back to Melbourne. Either way, it's a little bit of an undertaking, though a scenic one at that. If you have time, you might choose to stay overnight in pretty Port Campbell, 10 kilometres beyond the Twelve Apostles, before heading home.

Public transport along the GOW

Public transport is limited along the Great Ocean Road, which intersects with the GOW at Apollo Bay, Marengo, Princetown and the Twelve Apostles only — especially outside of the summer tourist season — reflecting its rural location and distance from populated areas. There are generally daily V/Line bus services on Mondays, Wednesdays and Fridays only. Ensure you check online at www.vline.com.au or call 1800 800 007 to check times for your specific dates and plan your journey before you travel. More details are in the back of this guide.

Shuttle services for day walkers

For those walking as a series of day walks and who do not have two cars to arrange their own car shuffle (nearest car access points for each day's walk start and finish are indicated in the 'Build your own walk' table), excellent private shuttle services are available but must be booked in advance — the transport operators are listed in the back of this book, and they can also arrange luggage transfer services so you only need walk with a day pack. Some accommodation providers also provide shuttle services for guests, where booked in advance. These are listed on pages 130 to 131, and were accurate at the time of printing, but circumstances change so do check first.

Camping and other accommodation

GOW has seven of the most spectacular, dedicated hikers-only campsites you could experience: they are hike-in/out only which makes for a lovely wild experience. They must be booked at least two weeks in advance (though in reality, much earlier if you don't want to risk being disappointed because they are booked out) with Parks Victoria: bookings.parks.vic.gov.au/great-ocean-walk.

Each campground has only 8 pitches each (each pitch suitable for a 2-3 person tent), usually with some additional small group sites. Groups of walkers using the individual pitches can be no more than 12 people, limited to a maximum of 4 pitches. Groups of up to 16 people may be accommodated in the dedicated small group camp areas at Elliot Ridge, Blanket Bay, Cape Otway, Aire River and Johanna Beach. Overnight walkers are required to register their trip (walking and camping) plans with Parks Victoria, for both safety and park management reasons, and this is done via the campground bookings.

Elliot Ridge campsite set up

Costs for the GOW Hikers walk in/out camps and nearby public Parks Victoria campsites vary. At the time of reprinting this guide, Parks Victoria are not charging for nearby sites (bookings are still required), although this may change, so make sure you check the most up-to-date information with Parks Victoria. Each hike-in site booked is for a maximum of 3 people. Carry your proof of booking with you, as Park Rangers can and do check permits when servicing the camps. Private campsites incur fees but offer more facilities.

GOW campgrounds are 'bushcamps' and have a single basic kitchen shelter (open air), small platforms for food prep, water tanks (water must be treated) and composting toilets — with some of the best views you will ever experience from a loo! The pitches are set well into the bush and are quite private. It is important to check with Parks Victoria as to the availability of water, which is rain dependent and not guaranteed. Use the tank water considerately and ensure you treat it before drinking. You must also carry out all of your rubbish. Be aware that at certain times of the year, mice can be persistent camping companions at some sites: come prepared to keep your food fully sealed and inside your tent (not in the fly/porch) in mice-proof containers. The campsites offer incredible views, lunch platforms, shelter and toilets (many with their own spectacular views!) for GOW day walkers as well, though priority should be given to booked campers and it is recommended you bring your own toilet paper in case it has run out.

Introduction

GOW Hikers campsites — must be prebooked

Day	Campground name	Notes
Day 1	Elliot Ridge GOW Campground	8 sites; 6 small group sites. Shelter, toilets, tables, untreated water. At top of long steady walk up Elliot Ridge. Hidden in the bush
Day 2	Blanket Bay GOW Campground	8 sites; 6 small group sites. Shelter, tables, untreated water. Toilets are a little walk further along in the public campground. At the base of the Katabanut Walk, beside Blanket Bay creek and before you enter the public campground.
Day 3	Cape Otway GOW campground	8 sites; 6 small group sites. Shelter, tables, toilet, untreated water. Just past the Cape Otway lightstation café – a bit of an incentive to arrive early so you can indulge in a scone and tea on the way to the campground (check if open).
Day 4	Aire River GOW Campground	8 sites; 6 small group sites. Shelter, tables, untreated water, toilets are available at neighbouring Aire River East public campground. Picturesque site beside Aire River, separate but beside public campground, so can be noisy.
Day 5	Johanna Beach GOW Campground	8 sites; no small group sites;groups can be accommodated at the public campgrounds. Shelter, table, toilet, untreated water. Spectacularly sited beyond Johanna Beach (public) Campground, atop a cliff-top hill beside the Old Coach Road, with big views and near to a walk-in hang-gliding launch spot.
Day 6	Ryans Den GOW Campground	8 sites; no small groups sites. Shelter, tables, untreated water, toilets. Another scenic site tucked off the main track with a beautiful lookout at the very end of the campsite. The view from the loo is spectacular.
Day 7	Devils Kitchen GOW Campground	8 sites; no small group sites. Shelter, tables, untreated water, toilets. If you take the Wreck Beach/Moonlight Beach option to see the wrecks (only possible at low tide), once you regain the main GOW track from the end of Moonlight Beach, you will have to walk back along the main track to enter Ryans Den. It is about the same distance as going the inland route, though the sand walking can be much slower going with heavy packs.

Other public camping

There are also some additional public camping sites along the way, which are generally larger and with car access, but still lovely and an alternative on some nights if GOW sites are fully booked. These are Parks Victoria or Great Ocean Road Authority sites unless otherwise indicated, and can be booked online www.parks.vic.gov.au/bookings .

Day	Campground name	Notes
Day 1	Marengo Family Caravan Park	Good facilities including amenity block, hot showers, camp kitchen, outdoor BBQ, laundry. Unpowered sites from $36/night. Bookings: www.marengo-caravanpark.com.au. Pretty though busy caravan park with quieter unpowered camping area at the back beside the GOW. Good for the night before the main walk if you arrive into Apollo Bay too late to do the full first day.
Day 2	Blanket Bay Campground	Picnic tables, firepits, untreated water, toilets, car park, beach and boat ramp. Right beside the beach – car access so can be very busy at peak times.
Day 3	Parker Hill Campground	20 sites, toilets, picnic tables (no water). At the top of the climb up from Parker Inlet with good views. The site is usually walk-in only (with the vehicle access track locked) so is relatively quiet.
Day 4	Aire River East Campground	20 sites, no amenities (available over bridge), car access. Sited beside pretty Aire River. Instead of crossing over the bridge at Aire River, walk straight ahead to the East campground.
Day 4	Aire River West Campground	40 sites, toilets, untreated water, fireplaces, car access. Sited on the opposite side of Aire River bridge. Popular campsite.
Day 5	Johanna Beach Camping Ground	25 sites, tables, toilets, untreated water, car park, no fires. Close to popular and beautiful Johanna Beach and lookouts.
Day 7	Princetown Recreation Reserve and Camping	Public sporting reserve which allows camping. Toilets, BBQ, laundry, playground, tennis court, car park. $10 per site per night, cash only, 3 nights minimum over Easter and long weekends. Bookings: call Mick on 0429 985176. Located beside Gellibrand River and the small village of Princetown (accessible via boardwalk on the other side of the river). Post Office and general store may or may not be open – phone ahead.

Other accommodation

There is a variety of accommodation available, from basic hostels and park cabins to luxury villas and glamping, for those who choose to take the daily shuttle approach, just walking with a day pack and enjoying a soft bed and warm shower at the end of each day. This is one of the attractions of the GOW for many — it still feels remote but is more accessible. Due to the road distances involved, many walkers choose to base themselves from two different locations, one for each half of the walk, so that they are not spending long distances each day in the car getting to/from the accommodation. Others prefer to base themselves centrally for the duration. Pages 130-131 lists accommodation options by area.

What to pack?

More experienced walkers will have their pack list well established, but if you are new to multi-day walking, here's some suggestions for what you might include.

Day walkers

If you are doing a series of day walks, you can happily carry a small day pack, with your luggage held at your accommodation. However, do remember that for most of the walk you will be quite remote, so still make sure you carry:

- ☐ A small first aid kit, including snake bandage (at least one per group)
- ☐ Blister care, if you are prone to blisters (or may be)
- ☐ Personal Locator Beacon (at least one per group) - mobile reception is patchy along the Walk
- ☐ Water bottles or bladder with sufficient water for the whole day (2-4 litres, depending on individual and temperature)
- ☐ Lunch and energy snacks
- ☐ Waterproof outer pants and jackets (even on sunny days)
- ☐ A warm layer (ditto!)
- ☐ Sunscreen
- ☐ Mosquito repellent (also good to discourage leeches)
- ☐ Hat
- ☐ Toilet paper and zip lock bag to carry it out
- ☐ Toilet trowel (one per group)
- ☐ GPS/Phone
- ☐ Camera
- ☐ Map & guidebook
- ☐ Head torch

Optional:

- ☐ Pocket knife (good for sliding leeches off!)
- ☐ Gaiters (snake/leech protection)
- ☐ Hiking poles
- ☐ Personal medications (including cooler travel cases for those needing to be kept cool)

Campers

Weight is definitely a consideration for most self-supporting walkers, and it is most definitely true that the lighter your pack, the more enjoyable your walk, but there can also be a trade-off between weight and comfort. Ultra-lightweight equipment can also be very expensive but may be worth the investment if you plan on doing more self-supporting walks. You can also hire gear from some tour operators and outdoor gear providers.

Introduction

In addition to the day-hiking pack list above:

- ☐ Backpack sufficient to hold your gear comfortably (remember it becomes part of the weight)
- ☐ Tent with fly
- ☐ Sleeping mat (including repair kit)
- ☐ Sleeping bag (recommended: 4 seasons)
- ☐ Clean fuel burning stove with fuel sufficient for entire walk (no shops along the way to refill and no open fires allowed)
- ☐ Cooking pot or billy
- ☐ Eating utensils
- ☐ Cleaning materials and environmentally friendly soap/detergent
- ☐ Zip lock bags or equivalent to carry out rubbish
- ☐ Water treatment system (steripens, filters, or water purification tablets such as Micropur Forte by Katadyn); Iodine is not recommended as it doesn't kill all the nasties and tastes terrible; boiling sufficient water for the 30 minutes needed will take more fuel than you are likely to be able to carry
- ☐ Internal drysac/heavy duty garbage bag to keep everything dry inside your pack
- ☐ Impermeable food storage containers to discourage mice
- ☐ A small portable radio to hear emergency broadcasts on AM774.

What to eat?
For those who are carrying all they need and camping each night, your body is carrying considerable weight and expending lots of energy each day for a week, so you will need to be fuelled with good, balanced nutrition to perform and recover well, but equally will need to take carrying weight into consideration. There are no stores along the route to restock with so you need to be fully self-sufficient for the entire walk. Dehydrated and vacuum-sealed pre-prepared meals are a good lightweight option. There are a number of good websites, active facebook groups and books which provide further detailed information and recipes for those who choose to be self-supporting, and it is worth experimenting in advance to find out what works for you if this is your first attempt.

Water
Ensure you carry sufficient drinking water for all walkers for each day. On hot days, this can be up to 1 litre an hour per person. If you feel thirsty, you are already dehydrated. If camping, it is important to check current water availability at each campsite with Parks Victoria before you walk, as it is not guaranteed. All water at the GOW campsites is untreated and MUST be treated before drinking/cooking. If you are new to water purification, you can find a good rundown of water purification/treatment options and pros and cons at www.australianhiker.com.au/advice/water-filtration.

To pole or not to pole?
This is arguably the most divisive topic amongst Aussie bushwalkers — whereas European walkers are not sure what all the fuss is about and use them from childhood onwards! Each to their own is our view. We are both keen hiking pole converts, finding them to provide good stability on some of the slippery downhills and creek crossings, taking pressure off creaky joints (particularly if you are carrying weight) and utilising the strength of arms — in addition to weary legs — to help get you up some of the long uphill sections. If you find it hard to get into the rhythm initially, track down some videos on-line (try: *how to use trekking poles like a pro*) and get out and practice.

With poles

Without poles

Caring for the environment

Almost all of the Great Ocean Walk traverses national parks and goes alongside marine sanctuaries. It is a precious landscape and environment which deserves our protection.

We advocate the minimal impact code of bushwalking to ensure our magnificent natural Australian bush and coastlines can be enjoyed by generations to come: *take nothing but photographs and leave nothing but footprints*. It's vital to avoid disturbing wildlife, leave cultural and heritage sites as you found them and dispose of your rubbish correctly. In designated marine sanctuaries, it is *illegal to remove shells and to fish*. You might even consider picking up any rubbish you come across (particularly plastics on beaches) and carrying it out.

The key principles are:

1. Plan ahead and prepare: bring enough food, water, sunscreen and clothing for your walk.
2. Walk on established tracks, even when wet and muddy. 'Going around' creates major erosion problems.
3. Dispose of waste responsibly – carry it in; carry it out.
4. Leave what you find – take only photographs and memories, leave only footprints. Do not disturb shells, wildlife or flora, cultural and/or historical artefacts. Take care not to walk off track beside the sea cliffs, where you may unwittingly disturb Aboriginal Middens and remnant areas of petrified forests.
5. Minimise campfire impacts – no campfires are permitted along the Great Ocean Walk. Campers are required to carry and use clean fuel stoves. On days of total fire ban, not even gas barbecues may be used.

6. Respect wildlife. Observe them from a distance and don't feed them. Store rations and rubbish securely.
7. Be considerate of other walkers and keep noise to a minimum. Be respectful of other users of the land and don't climb fences or scare stock.
8. If you absolutely cannot wait for the designated toilet facilities (at the GOW and public campsites) and you just have to go, dig a hole at least 20 centimetre deep and at least 100 metres (preferably 200 metres) away from water and the track. Carry a small hand shovel in your group for this purpose. Cover it up when finished and carry out all toilet paper and sanitary products in a zip-lock bag. Australia's burrowing marsupials are keen diggers and the last thing anyone wants is a beautiful GOW spoiled with toilet paper.

Phytophthora cinnamomi (cinnamon fungus or dieback) – boot cleaning

At various points along the GOW, you will find boot cleaning stations designed to try and slow the spread of *Phytophera* ('fye-tof-ra') disease (cinnamon root rot), a plant pathogen which can have devastating effects on the beautiful habitat and, in particular, Australian grass trees which are a feature of the walk. You will see some areas where the long fronds of the grass trees have turned brown and crumbled away, and given these trees only grow at the pace of 1-6 centimetres a year and some are over 400 years old, this is just tragic to see. It is spread through the movement of infected soil, water or plant material, including on hiking boots and equipment (including walking poles). Please use every single cleaning station diligently — kick your boots back and forth through the brushes to take any dirt and mud off the sole and sides, then dip your boots in and out of the detergent via the cleaning plates. Do the same with the tips of your poles.

Not walking with your dog

As the Great Ocean Walk traverses a number of national and marine parks, dogs are not permitted along the walk.

Emergencies

Be aware that mobile phone coverage can be patchy on some of the more remote sections on the walk. In general, Telstra offers better coverage than Optus, but it cannot be relied on in an emergency. Carrying a small PLB (Personal Locator Beacon) should really be a given, and if you don't already have one they can be hired from a number of outdoor providers.

We encourage all walkers to complete a *trip intentions form*, which details your plans, and leave this with a trusted friend, family or responsible authority, who can raise the alarm if you do not return as planned. Do remember to let them know when you have finished! You can download one from www.police.vic.gov.au/outdoor-and-bush-safety . If you are camping at the GOW campgrounds, you will be required to provide similar information, including an emergency contact person, as part of the registration and booking process.

We have listed possible access/exit points for the walk in the 'Build Your Own Walk' table. If something goes wrong but you are able to safely walk out along one of these to a vehicle access track, it will make getting emergency services to you more quickly, providing you can give exact details of your location. Along the walk route itself, you will find green GOW emergency beacon posts with a dedicated number (starting from GOW001 at Marengo). If you do find yourself with an emergency requiring outside help, and cannot provide your GPS location to the emergency service or via a PLB, being able to provide them with correct directions/distance from the nearest locator number will greatly assist them in getting to you quickly. You will find further information in the back of the book under 'Safety Tips'.

Bushfires and track closures

In recent years, fire and floods have damaged many walking tracks in Victoria, including along the Great Ocean Road, although luckily the Great Ocean Walk route has been largely unaffected to date. It is not uncommon during hot summer days for total fire bans to be imposed, so please monitor the situation closely. When a 'Code Red' fire rating is announced, most of the region's state and national parks will be closed for public safety: monitor http://parkweb.vic.gov.au/safety/fire,-flood-and-other-closures and be aware you may need to change your plans at short notice. Many Australians have recent experience of how fast and unpredictably bushfires can burn, with embers lighting spot fires kilometres ahead of fire fronts, so please follow any directions given by local authorities. Having ourselves been evacuated from the Kangaroo Island Wilderness Trail at dawn on the morning of the devastating bushfires in 2019, we cannot stress enough how important it is to follow local advice and official guidance in this respect. If you are unavoidably trapped along the GOW by a fire, the best advice is to try and let emergency services know your location (though they may not be able to come and get you immediately if it is not safe to do so), wear your merino/wool clothing to help provide some protection for your skin, get down to the lowest point possible or a large open, cleared or rocky area where available, which may be by the water if that is safe. You cannot outrun a bushfire, so the focus is on getting to the safest possible location — and to avoid being caught in the first place.

At a Glance: Itinerary Options

The GOW directions in this book follow the 'official' 8-day route set out in the official Parks Victoria map. However, we have also suggested itineraries for shorter or longer options below, depending on how much distance you prefer to cover in a day. We have also detailed a 'Build Your Own Walk' table which lists every entry and exit point along the walk for those who wish to customise their own itineraries. Finally, we recommend purchasing a copy of the *Great Ocean Walk Information Guide & Official Map* (6th or subsequent editions) to supplement this guide. This can sometimes be a bit hard to find locally, so may be best purchase online in advance rather than relying on it being available on arrival at Apollo Bay, though the Visitor Information Centre tries to keep it in stock.

Walks at a glance

CAMPERS OPTIONS

8 day itinerary (Camping) - RECOMMENDED BY PARKS VIC

Day	From	To	Distance
Day 1	Apollo Bay Visitor Centre	Elliot Ridge GOW Campground	9.8 km
Day 2	Elliot Ridge GOW Campground	Blanket Bay GOW Campground	11.8 km
Day 3	Blanket Bay GOW Campground	Cape Otway GOW Campground	10.5 km
Day 4	Cape Otway GOW Campground	Aire River GOW Campground	9.5 km
Day 5	Aire River GOW Campground	Johanna Beach GOW Campground	13.6 km
Day 6	Johanna Beach GOW Campground	Ryans Den GOW Campground	13.6 km
Day 7	Ryans Den GOW Campground	Devils Kitchen GOW Campground	13.4 km
Day 8	Devils Kitchen GOW Campground	Twelve Apostles Visitor Info Centre	15.2 km
			97.4 km

Note: No rounding of distances, so varies slightly from official GOW Map distances

6 day itinerary (Camping)

Day	From	To	Distance
Day 1	Apollo Bay Visitor Centre	Blanket Bay GOW Campground	21.6 km
Day 2	Blanket Bay GOW Campground	Aire River GOW Campground	20.0 km
Day 3	Aire River GOW Campground	Johanna Beach GOW Campground	13.6 km
Day 4	Johanna Beach GOW Campground	Ryans Den GOW Campground	13.6 km
Day 5	Ryans Den GOW Campground	Devils Kitchen GOW Campground	13.4 km
Day 6	Devils Kitchen GOW Campground	Twelve Apostles Visitor Info Centre	15.2 km
			97.4 km

4 day itinerary (Camping)

Day	From	To	Distance
Day 1	Apollo Bay Visitor Centre	Blanket Bay GOW Campground	21.6 km
Day 2	Blanket Bay GOW Campground	Aire River GOW Campground	20.0 km
Day 3	Aire River GOW Campground	Ryans Den GOW Campground	27.2 km
Day 4	Ryans Den GOW Campground	Twelve Apostles Visitor Info Centre	28.6 km
			97.4 km

DAY WALKERS OPTIONS

8 day itinerary (day walkers)

Day	From	To	Distance
Day 1	Apollo Bay Visitor Centre	Shelley Beach Picnic Area car park	8.3 km
Day 2	Shelly Beach Picnic Area car park	Blanket Bay campground car park	13.3 km
Day 3	Blanket Bay Campground car park	Cape Otway Light Station car park	9.9 km
Day 4	Cape Otway Light Station car park	Aire River car park	9.9 km
Day 5	Aire River car park	Johanna Beach car park	13.2 km
Day 6	Johanna Beach car park	Ryans Den Track/GOR	14.3 km
Day 7	Ryans Den Track/GOR	Wreck Beach car park	12.4 km
Day 8	Wreck Beach car park	Twelve Apostles Visitor Info Centre	18.1 km
			99.4 km

Note: Or can stop at Princetown (11.2 km) and do Day 9 to Twelve Apostles (6.9 km) in time for afternoon bus.

5 day itinerary (day walkers)

Day	From	To	Distance
Day 1	Apollo Bay Visitor Centre	Blanket Bay Campground Car park	21.6 km
Day 2	Blanket Bay Campground car park	Aire River car park	19.8 km
Day 3	Aire River car park	3 Ways (Hider Access Rd)	18.2 km
Day 4	3 Ways (Hider Access Rd)	The Gable car park	18.5 km
Day 5	The Gable car park	Twelve Apostles Visitor Info Centre	19.3 km
			97.4 km

4 day itinerary (day walkers)

Day	From	To	Distance
Day 1	Apollo Bay Visitor Centre	Blanket Bay Campground car park	21.6 km
Day 2	Blanket Bay Campground car park	Aire River Campground car park	19.8 km
Day 3	Aire River Campground car park	Ryans Den Track access at GOR	27.5 km
Day 4	Ryans Den Track access from GOR	Twelve Apostles Visitor Info Centre	30.5 km
			99.4 km

Walks at a glance

'Build your own Walk' distance and access points table

Day (Parks Vic Guide)	From	To
Day 1	Apollo Bay Visitor Centre	Marengo Holiday Park
	Marengo	Shelley Beach Picnic Area
	Shelley Beach Picnic Area	Eliot Ridge GOW Campground
Day 2	Eliot Ridge GOW Campground	Blanket Bay GOW Campground
Day 3	Blanket Bay GOW Campground	Parker Inlet
	Parker Inlet	Parker Hill Campground
	Parker Hill Campground	Cape Otway Lightstation
	Cape Otway Lightstation	Cape Otway GOW Campground
Day 4	Cape Otway GOW Campground	Aire River GOW Campground
Day 5	Aire River GOW Campground	Castle Cove Lookout
	Castle Cove Lookout	Johanna Beach GOW Campground
Day 6	Johanna Beach GOW Campground	3 Ways (Hiders Access Rd)
	3 Ways (Hider Access Rd)	Milanesia Beach
	Melanesia Beach	Ryans Den Track turn off
	Ryans Den Track turn off	Ryans Den GOW Campground
Day 7	Ryans Den GOW Campground	Parkers Access Road
	Parkers Access Road	The Gable car park
	The Gable car park	Wreck Beach car park
	Wreck Beach car park	Devils Kitchen GOW Campground
Day 8	Devils Kitchen GOW Campground	Gellibrand River car park
	Gellibrand River car park	Gibson Steps
	Gibson Steps	Twelve Apostles

Distance	Transport Access/Exit Point
3.0 km	Yes (Marengo beach car park)
5.3 km	Yes (Shelley Beach car park via Elliot River Road)
via River 1.5 km via Inland 2.5 km	No
11.8 km	Yes (Blanket Bay Campground car park via Blanket Bay Road, off Lighthouse Road (to Cape Otway))
4.3 km	No
0.4 km	Yes (Parker Hill Track or Crayfish Bay Track via Blanket Bay Road)
5.2 km	Yes (Cape Otway car park via Lighthouse Road)
0.6 km	Yes (Cape Otway car park via Lighthouse Road)
9.5 km	Yes (Aire River Campground via Hordon Vale Rd, off GOR) or Sand Road at Glenaire (Seasonally closed)
6.0 km	Yes - Castle Cove Lookout car park (on GOW at Glenaire)
7.6 km	Yes - Johanna Beach car park via Johanna Road
4.4 km	Yes - (junction of Hiders Access and Melanesia Track)
4.7 km	No
3.6 km	Yes- Ryans Den Track (additional 1 km walk off GOR to locked gate on GOW - very limited parking)
0.9 km	No
5.1 km	Yes - Parkers Access Road (dry weather only for vehicles, otherwise 1.5 km uphill walk to Moonlight Head Road)
4.2 km	Yes - via Moonlight Head Road
1.2 km	Yes - Via Wreck Beach Rd, off Moonlight Head Road
Beach or inland 2.9 km	No
8.3 km	Yes - via Old Coach Rd, near Princetown
5.8 km	Yes - Gibson Steps car park
1.1 km	Yes - Twelve Apostles Visitor Centre

A trudge along Station Beach

Bald Hill

Day 1 Apollo Bay to Elliot Ridge/Shelly Beach

The first day of the Great Ocean Walk (GOW) starts with a flat walk along a path along Mounts Bay and beside the Great Ocean Road, from the Tourist Information Centre in Apollo Bay to Marengo Caravan Park. It's an unassuming start, but soon leaves the town and houses behind to follow along rolling hills for varied and wonderful views, optional routes (at low tide only) along the rock platforms and beaches, and a pretty river crossing with stepping stones. If tides are high and the Elliot River crossing isn't possible, there is a lovely and easy alternate inland route through lush fern gullies. For those camping, there is a lung-busting final slog up Elliot Ridge to reach the first of the spectacular GOW walker-only campgrounds. Day walkers save that joy for the start of their second day when their legs are fresh, instead exiting early at Shelly Beach car park.

At a glance

Distance: 9.8 km (camping), 8.3 km (day walk)

Time: approx. 3.5 hours

Difficulty: Medium

Highlights: Views, Elliot River crossing, Shelly Beach

Start of the Great Ocean Walk

Do check your tide times and plan your day accordingly, as there are three short beach sections during the day which do not have alternative inland options, so you should be aiming for a low or outgoing tide for this section. Very experienced and fit walkers sometimes opt to combine days 1 and 2 (22 kilometres through to Blanket Bay), but the gentler start suits many people arriving into Apollo Bay in the morning and starting the walk on the same day. Alternate route options (Decision Points) are detailed in the table after the walk directions, and are signposted on the walk.

Day 1 Apollo Bay to Elliot Ridge/Shelly Beach

Supplies

Apollo Bay is a popular seaside tourist town which has a lovely patrolled (in season) surf beach, weekly markets, and a good range of accommodation for those arriving the day before they start the Walk. It's worth staying longer if you have the time. There is also a good range of shops, cafés and a small IGA supermarket suitable for last minute stock ups – the last until you get to Port Campbell after the end of the walk and only if it is open! The next coffee is not until the Cape Otway Lightstation café, three days away! The friendly Apollo Bay Tourist Information Centre, which is the official start of the Walk, offers excellent information about the area. The bus stop is just in front of it.

	Start	Finish	
Camping Option	Apollo Bay Visitors Centre	Elliot Ridge GOW Campground	9.8 km
Day Walk Option	Apollo Bay Visitors Centre	Shelly Beach Picnic Ground car park	8.3 km

Walk directions

1.1 From the Tourist Information Centre, the Walk commences south towards Marengo, parallel to the beach and main shopping street, following the footpath along to the beach side of the Great Ocean Road (B100). The beach will be on your left. Head out of town, past the sporting fields, cross the Barham River then continue alongside Mounts Bay where the sealed footpath becomes gravel. Look out for the

Across the rock platforms

Day 1 Apollo Bay to Elliot Ridge/Shelly Beach

Australian fur seals you can sometimes see on the offshore rocks as you approach Hayley Point (Cape Marengo).

Inland and beach options

1.2 At the end of the pedestrian footpath (as the Great Ocean Road curves away from the beach) turn left through the Marengo Beach car park and go straight ahead to enter the Marengo Holiday (caravan) Park – look for the green GOW sign on the left. Pass through the entry gate and follow the main road through the Holiday Park. It curves around to a sign (‘*camping unpowered*’) with a small GOW flash – it’s easy to miss. Walk through the grassed camping area and then through the gate, which is well signed for the GOW. The grassy track takes you away from the park and along the foreshore, in front of some houses and then past farmland. You are away! (*At low tide only*: instead of going through

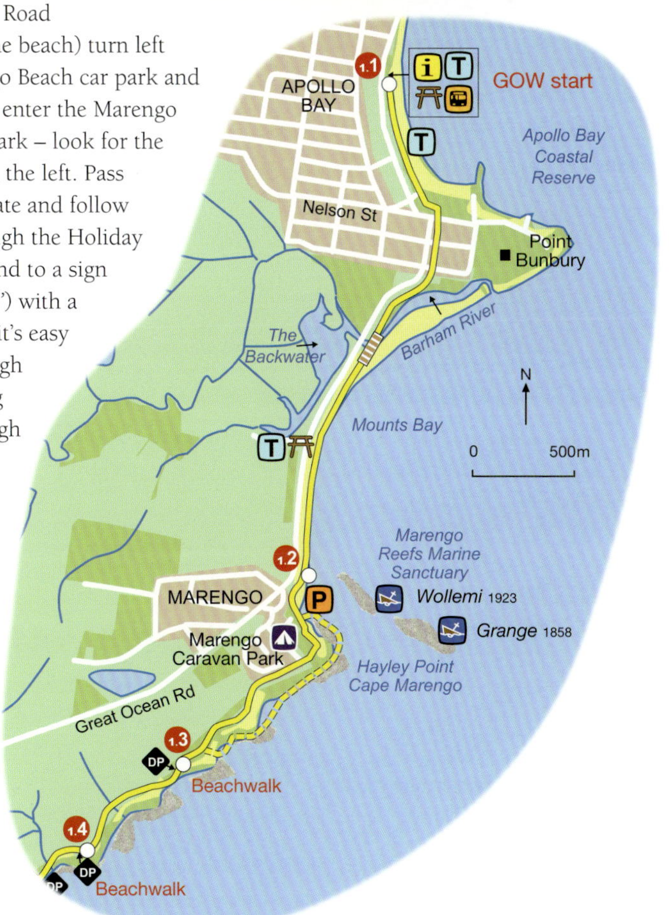

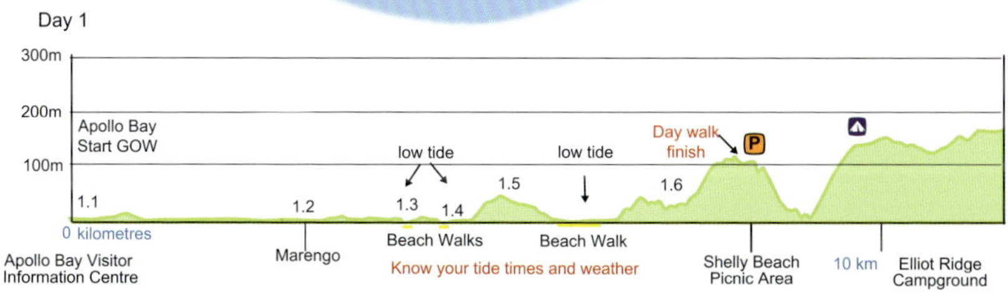

Day 1 Apollo Bay to Elliot Ridge/Shelly Beach

Heading off from Marengo

Beach walk section at Three Creeks

the holiday park you can opt to go down onto the beach via the ramp on the left just before the Park entrance, to walk on the flat rock platforms around the headland and along the beach, re-joining the main path at the end of the beach.)

1.3 The path descends to the eastern end of the next beach which is **Decision Point 1** (Storm Point). There is no inland/highwater alternative, so ensure you are there at an outgoing/low tide, watch for unexpected waves and walk the easy 200 metres to the end of the beach to re-join the GOW at **Decision Point 1A** (signed). It is recommended that you take the inland option here.

1.4 The inland path continues to **Decision Point 1B**, where it drops along another unnamed beach for 200 metres. If the tide is in, you may have to wait for the water to recede before proceeding. At the end of the beach, at Bald Hill (**Decision Point 2**), the inland option is advised and a long steady walk up Bald Hill rewards with vast views – a good excuse to stop and catch your breath at the top.

Day 1 Apollo Bay to Elliot Ridge/Shelly Beach

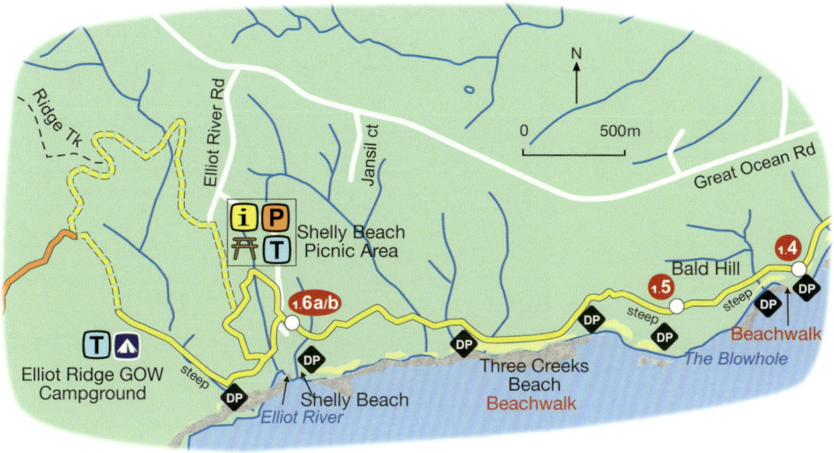

1.5 From the top of the hill, continue down to Three Creeks Beach (**Decision Point 2B**), walking 600 metres to its end if the tide is out – there is no inland option. The sign at the end of the beach (**Decision Point 3**) indicates the recommended inland route. This takes you into sheltered coastal scrub and low trees bent by the constant winds, crossing damp fern gullies with glimpses down to the ocean.

Through the fern gullies

1.6a At the signed junction to Shelly Creek, it's worth taking the 100-metre detour down to Shelly Beach for a nice stop and to explore the rockpools. **IF YOU ARE A DAY WALKER**, at the Shelly Beach track junction turn right to go up the hill through fern gullies to the Shelly Beach Picnic Area and carpark for pick up.

1.6b **IF YOU ARE CAMPING**, continue straight ahead at the Shelly Beach track junction for another 1.5 kilometres, descending steeply down to Elliot River to cross the stepping stones then turn right to start the long slog up Elliot Ridge to reach the GOW campground at the top.

The long haul up to Elliot Ridge campsite

As the track levels out, at the T-junction, turn left to reach the campground. If Elliot River is flooded and unpassable or you want a gentler end to the day, you can take the pretty inland option accessed via the turnoff along the road 370 metres beyond the Shelly Beach Picnic Area (see inland option p37) which avoids the long haul up Elliot Ridge but is 800 metres longer than the main Elliot River route.

Elliot River crossing

Marengo Reefs Marine Sanctuary and Southern Bull Kelp

Just 150 metres off the shoreline at Cape Marengo (waypoint 1.2), lies the 12-hectare marine sanctuary which protects Little Henty Reef. Part of the Otway Marine Bioregion, the inner and outer sandstone reefs are often exposed at low tide, separated by a narrow channel ('The Gap'). While it looks fairly innocuous, the *Grange* was shipwrecked on this reef in 1858 and the *Wollemi* in 1923. Despite this history, the inter-tidal and sub-tidal reefs are home to a rich and biodiverse eco-system, including soft corals, sea urchins, sponge gardens, abalone, sea snails and crabs, as well as hosting a colony of sea lions on the visible outcrop. The deeper waters (to 6 metres) along this shoreline contain huge forests of dark brown southern Bull Kelp seaweed (*Durvilleae potatorum*- named after French botanist and explorer, Jules Sebastien Cesar Dumont d'Urville, 1790-1842). The leathery kelp is found all along the Southern Ocean shores and was purportedly used by Aboriginal Tasmanians and the Maori in New Zealand to make clothing, footwear and food bags. You will often see it washed up on the beaches along the Walk after storms.

Alternate routes

Parks Victoria *recommends the use of only the* ***GOW inland*** *route options where these options are available*. Alternate routes along the beaches and rock platforms can be interesting but should only be attempted at low tide (preferably outgoing) in calm weather and may involve exposure to dangerous (including freak) waves, currents, tides, rock scrambling, gullies, poor sightlines and limited or no escape options. We have walked each of the options listed below at low tide and provide a quick outline of what you might expect. Where it is quite unwise, regardless of tides, even for experienced and highly capable walkers, we have listed as 'not recommended'. Decision Point numbering aligns with the official map and the signage. They are shown as DP on our maps.

GOW Official Decision Point	Description/location	Conditions	Exit/escape options
n/a	Cape Marengo, in front of and before entering the holiday park. Access via ramp onto beach.	Flat rock platforms uncovered at low tide. Some sandy beach. Easy walking.	Good: a number of easy tracks up from the beaches along the way.
Storm Point Decision Point **1**	Unnamed beach walk.	Flat sandy beach. Easy walking if tide is out.	**No inland option.** May need to wait for water to recede. No exit for 200 m.
Storm Point Decision Point **1A**	End of beach (1 above) access.	Rock platforms. Rock scrambling required. Regularly covered by rising tides and waves.	Not recommended. No exit for 500 m.
Storm Point Decision Point **1B**	Unnamed beach walk.	Flat sandy beach. Easy walking if tide is out.	**No inland option.** May need to wait for water to recede. No exit for 200 m.
Bald Hill Decision Point **2**	At end of beach (1B above).	Deep rock gutters, scrambling, poor sightlines, frequent waves, cliffs with no escape options.	Not recommended. No exit for 1100 m.
Bald Hill Decision Point **2A**	Unsigned grassy path leading off to the left as you start to descend Bald Hill.	Deep rock gutters, scrambling, poor sightlines, frequent waves, cliffs with no escape options.	Not recommended. No exit for 450 m.
Bald Hill Decision Point **2B**	Eastern end of Three Creeks Beach.	Flat sandy beach. Easy walking if tide is out.	**No inland option.** May need to wait for water to recede. No exit for 600 m.
Three Creeks Decision Point **3**	Western end of Three Creeks Beach.	Rock platforms often covered in water, rock gutters, rock scrambling, poor sightlines.	Not recommended. No exit for 1500 m.
Shelly Beach Decision Point **4**	Shelly Beach (100 m detour from main track).	Rock platforms often covered in water, rock gutters, rock scrambling, poor sightlines.	Not recommended. No exit until you reach Elliot River mouth (400 m).

GOW Official Decision Point	Description/location	Conditions	Exit/escape options
Shelly Beach Picnic Area Inland Option	From Shelly Beach Picnic Area, walk back up gravel vehicle road for about 370 m. Entrance is to the left, past the locked gate - follow the path keeping an eye out for the GOW markers.	Easy walking along dirt vehicle access tracks through pretty fern gullies. Avoids Elliot River crossing if tide is high, as well as the long haul up to Elliot Ridge. Similar distance to river route.	Not required.
Elliot River Decision Point **5**	Elliot River mouth (only for those continuing onto Blanket Bay instead of finishing the day at Elliot Ridge GOW campground).	Dangerous and extended exposed rock platforms, often covered with water, with cliffs and limited exit options. Deep gutters, scrambling, frequent waves and poor sightlines.	*Seriously* not recommended.

Marengo rock platforms at low tide

Southern Right Whales

Between June and September, you may be lucky enough to spot Southern Right Whales (*Eubalaena australis*), including calves, from this open vantage point. Further along the coast, past the Twelve Apostles, at Warnambool, is a major calving ground or 'nursery' and maternal whales return here on average every 3 years. Calves will stay with their mothers for the first year of their lives. It is thought that the rough waters of the Southern coasts provide a type of sonic protection for the whales and their calves, disguising their sounds from potential predators. Southern Right Whales are one of three baleen (whalebone) whales and were known as Right Whales because they were the 'right whales' to slaughter. The

whaling industry thrived along this part of the Victorian Coast until the taking of Southern Right Whales was banned in Australia and New Zealand in 1935 because of a plummeting population of them (whaling in Australia actually continued until 1978). More than 26,000 southern right whales had been taken in Australian and New Zealand waters between 1822 and 1930. Not surprisingly, given the whaling industry impacts, while numbers are growing, there are still relatively few whales in Victorian waters, with only 300 individuals being monitored regularly along this coastline, compared to almost 3500 in southwestern waters. Some trivia night facts: adult females can weigh up to 80 tonnes, reach 18 metres in length and live for up to 100 years. They feed almost exclusively on zooplankton (krill), and the testicles of male right whales are the largest of any animal on earth, weighing up to 500 kg each!

Day 2 Elliot Ridge/Shelly Beach to Blanket Bay

At a glance

Distance: 11.8 km (camping), 13.3 km (day walk)

Time: approx. 4.5 hours

Difficulty: Medium, can be very muddy when wet

Highlights: Inland route through tall eucalypts and rainforests, Elliot River crossing, Blanket Bay

The walk from Shelly Beach to Blanket Bay is quite different to the rest of the walk, as it travels inland through dense forests of towering mountain ash (*Eucalyptus regnans*), the tallest flowering plant in the world. Valued for their straight thick trunks, the trees can grow to over 110 metres and have consequently been logged since the 1850s, used for railways and housing. Springboard holes were cut into the trunks to allow the timber cutters to get above the thick buttressed bases to make it easier to saw and chop. You can still find evidence of this method of tree felling in massive old moss covered stumps on the side of the track. As the track loops back towards the ocean, the eucalypts give way to coastal vegetation. Sections of this walk can be very muddy and slippery in the wet, and the Elliot River crossing may not be passable after very heavy rain, requiring you to use the inland alternate route. For those camping, ensure your food storage is rodent proof, as mice or bush rats can be enthusiastic night raiders at the Blanket Bay campground.

Rock shelf at Blanket Bay

Day 2 Elliot Ridge/Shelly Beach to Blanket Bay

	Start	Finish	
Camping Option	Elliot Ridge GOW Campground, Waypoint 2.3	Blanket Bay GOW Campground	11.8 km
Day walk option	Shelly Beach picnic ground	Blanket Bay Campground car park	13.3 km

Walk directions

2.1 FOR DAY WALKERS, start from the Shelly Beach car park and follow the GOW trail markers until you reach the sign to *Elliot River*, then turn right to walk down the path. As it winds down hill there are occasional glimpses of the ocean. On reaching the river take great care crossing on the stepping stones. After heavy rain, the river may be too dangerous to cross and the alternate inland path (accessed via the road from the Shelly Beach Picnic Area), through the rainforest and fern gullies, should be taken.

Stepping stones across Elliot River

2.2 Once you are on the opposite bank, turn right and walk up hill. The walk continues steeply upwards along Elliot Ridge before evening out to a gentle climb through ferns, tall eucalypts then coastal forest, beech, blanket leaf and stringy bark trees.

2.3 Upon reaching the T-junction, turn right to follow the walk marker and the sign *to Elliot River Loop walk* (turning left takes you to the Elliot Ridge GOW Campground). FOR CAMPERS, start the day here by leaving the campground to re-join the main GOW track and continue straight ahead.

Day 2 Elliot Ridge/Shelly Beach to Blanket Bay

The walk continues steeply upwards

2.4 When you reach the Y-junction, take the left 4WD track to follow the signs to *Blanket Bay GOW campground*. This wide track undulates through dense bush, ferns and tall mountain ash, the world's tallest flowering plant, reaching heights of 114 metres. The track can be muddy after rain.

2.5 Turn left at the junction of Elliot Road and Parker Road, following the sign to *Blanket Bay GOW Campground*. This is also a good place to have a break before setting off again.

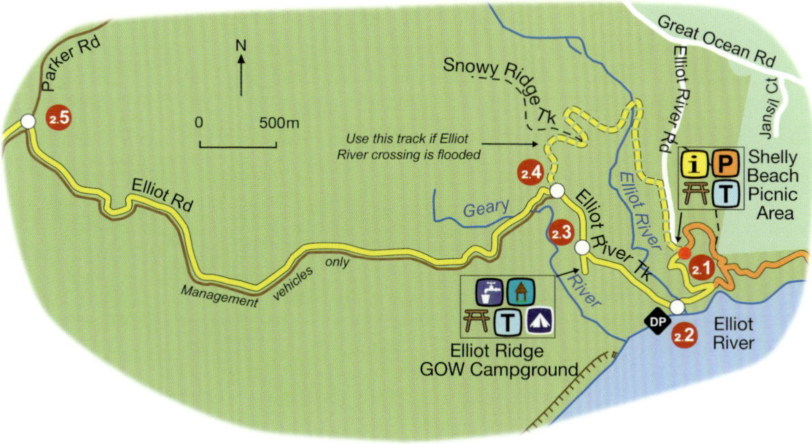

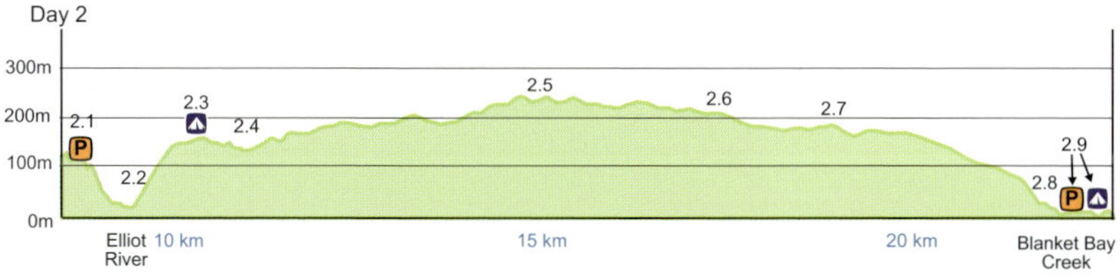

Day 2 Elliot Ridge/Shelly Beach to Blanket Bay

Follow the sign to Blanket Bay

2.6 At the intersection of Parker Road and Johnson Track, turn left and follow the GOW marker *to Blanket Bay campground*. Look out for the big old tree stump on the left with the timber-cutters' springboard holes. The vegetation changes along here from rainforest to coastal melaleuca, white bearded and pink heaths.

2.7 At the signed *Blanket Bay track*, turn right following the yellow GOW marker to *Blanket Bay* and continue until you reach Telegraph track. Follow the path around to the left towards Blanket Bay and the signed *GOW campground 2.1 km*. The track narrows as you gently descend and the vegetation once again changes to tall eucalyptus and open woodland. As the track rounds a bend to the right and goes steeply down stone steps, you can finally catch glimpses of the beach and hear the waves breaking on the shore.

2.8 At the bottom of the steps, turn sharp left past the yellow trail marker and along the rough, slippery, narrow path. As you near the bottom of the hill, take the path off to the left down to the beach and Blanket Bay (**Decision Point 6**). If the tide is too high to walk along the beach, take the alternative inland route which is signposted as *Katabanut Walk*. At the bottom of the stairs do a short detour and turn left along the beach for about 20 metres, look up to the left to see the ruined

Springboard holes cut into the timber

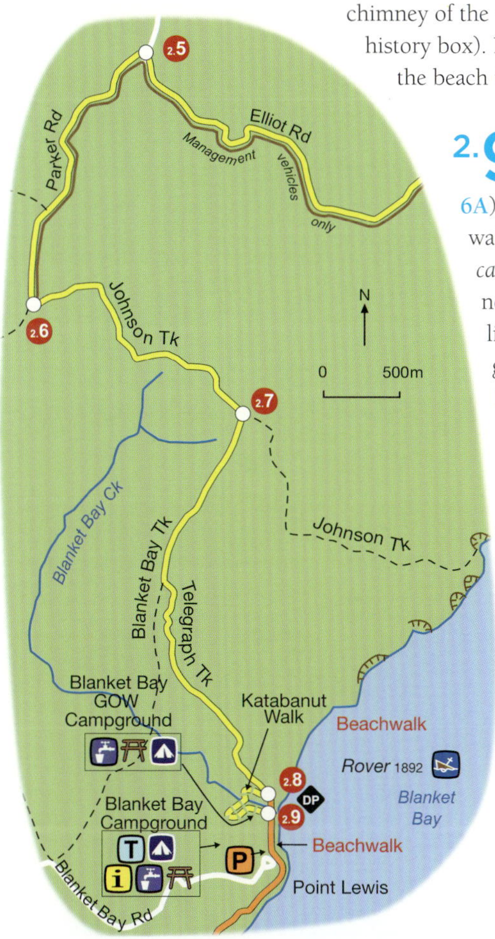

chimney of the old lighthouse storage shed (see history box). Retrace your steps and walk along the beach if the tide is low.

2.9 **FOR CAMPERS**, at the first set of steps (**Decision Point 6A**), cross Blanket Bay Creek and walk up to the *Blanket Bay GOW campground*. This is situated right next to the beach. There's a beautiful little waterfall near campsite 2, a good place to sit and contemplate. **FOR DAY WALKERS**, continue along the beach to **Decision Point 6B** to walk up the path to the Day Visitor's car park for pick-up.

Alternate routes

Parks Victoria recommends the use of only the ***GOW inland*** route options where these options are available. Alternate routes along the beaches and rock platforms can be interesting but should only be attempted at low tide (preferably outgoing) in calm weather and may involve exposure to dangerous (including freak) waves, currents, tides, rock scrambling, gullies, poor sightlines and limited or no escape options. Where it is quite unwise, regardless of tides, even for experienced and highly capable walkers, we have listed as 'not recommended'. Decision Point names/numbering aligns with the official map and signage.

GOW Official Decision Point	Description/location	Conditions	Exit/escape options
Elliot River Decision Point **5**	Elliot River mouth to Blanket Bay via rock platforms (only for those continuing onto Blanket Bay instead of finishing day at Elliot Ridge GOW campground).	Dangerous and extended, exposed rock platforms (often covered with water), with cliffs and limited exit options. Deep gutters, scrambling, frequent waves and poor sightlines.	*Seriously* not recommended. Use inland route.
Blanket Bay Decision Point **6**	Where GOW track meets the beach.	Easy walk along 200 metres of beach instead of the inland walk via the campground. You may need to wade across Blanket Bay Creek after rain or a high tide to reach the GOW campground.	Katabanut Walk is the inland detour if needed.
Blanket Bay Decision Point **6A**	Blanket Bay Beach on the south side of Blanket Bay Creek.	Easy short walk parallel to the GOW along the beach past the boat ramp.	Easy.
Blanket Bay Decision Point **6B**	Blanket Bay to Parker River via rock platforms.	Extended rock platforms and deep gullies. Requires scrambling. Impassable on rising tides and high seas.	*Seriously* not recommended. Use inland route. No exit points before Parker Inlet.

The waterfall at the rear of Blanket Bay campground

Sunrise over Blanket Bay

A brief history of Blanket Bay

In the late 1870s, Blanket Bay was chosen as an alternative to the treacherous waters of Parker River for the drop off point for the delivery of provisions to the Cape Otway Lightstation. An overland bullock track to the lighthouse was constructed and in the 1880s a new jetty (the remains of which can still be seen at very low tide) and stone supply huts were built. The ruins of the buildings are clearly visible just off the beach to the east of the track and next to the eastern side of the creek where there is another small cluster of ruined buildings. Despite it being more protected than the bay at Parker Inlet, in 1896 it was the scene of what would become known as the Blanket Bay Disaster and would eventually lead to the sea supply route being replaced by rail and road. Three crew members of the supply ship *Lady Loch* were drowned whilst manoeuvring one of the tender boats through the gap in the reef. Meanwhile the Captain and the lighthouse Superintendent were enjoying a brandy below decks, oblivious to the unfolding tragedy.

Cape Otway Lightstation

Day 3 Blanket Bay to Cape Otway

At a glance

Distance: 10.5 km (camping), 9.9 km (day walk)

Time: 3 hours

Difficulty: Medium

Highlights: Forests, Parker Inlet River crossing, lookouts, Cape Otway Lightstation

This is another day of revelations, with the walk/wade across the Parker River Inlet a highlight: it should not be attempted at high or on an incoming tide with rolling waves when the water can be head high or above, so it's good to time this day's walk around the tide times. Another incentive to cross at very low tide is that you may also be able to see, embedded in the sand, the very last remains of the shipwreck of the American-built wooden sailboat *Eric the Red*, which was travelling from New York to Melbourne in 1880 before it was wrecked on the Otway Reef. There is a steep haul up to Parker Hill before the day finishes, with a walk above Crayfish Bay into the spectacular and historic Cape Otway lightstation, home to Australia's oldest and most significant lighthouse.

Eric the Red's Anchor

Day 3 Blanket Bay to Cape Otway

	Start	Finish	
Camping option	Blanket Bay GOW Campground	Cape Otway GOW Campground	10.5 km
Day walk option	Blanket Bay Campground car park	Cape Otway Lightstation car park	9.9 km

Heading uphill

Walk directions

3.1 FOR CAMPERS, set off along the GOW route, through the Blanket Bay public camping area/car park (or along the Blanket Bay beach past the boat ramp before rejoining at Decision Point 6B).

FOR DAY WALKERS, pick up the GOW boardwalk to the right of the information board in the Blanket Bay Campground car park. Make sure you use the boot hygiene cleaning station and continue straight ahead to climb gently through the woodland.

View to Parker Inlet

3.2 Take the signed detour a short 170 metres off to the left to Point Lewis lookout, which offers a picnic table and beautiful views. Once back on the main track, turn left to continue uphill through stringybark forests and grasstrees, crossing little footbridges along the way. The track descends via a viewpoint to the Parker River inlet.

3.3 Cross the inlet at low/outgoing tide only, aiming for the opposite river bank above the sand dunes. This is not a place to take risks. You are likely to get wet unless the tide is very low. As you cross the river, look towards the sea, and watch for the remnant timbers of the *Eric the Red* shipwreck, which are sometimes exposed on the left-hand side of the beach near the shoreline. From the other side of the river, walk to the right beside the river until the path starts to climb for a long steady pull up stone stairs to the top of Parker Hill.

Day 3 Blanket Bay to Cape Otway

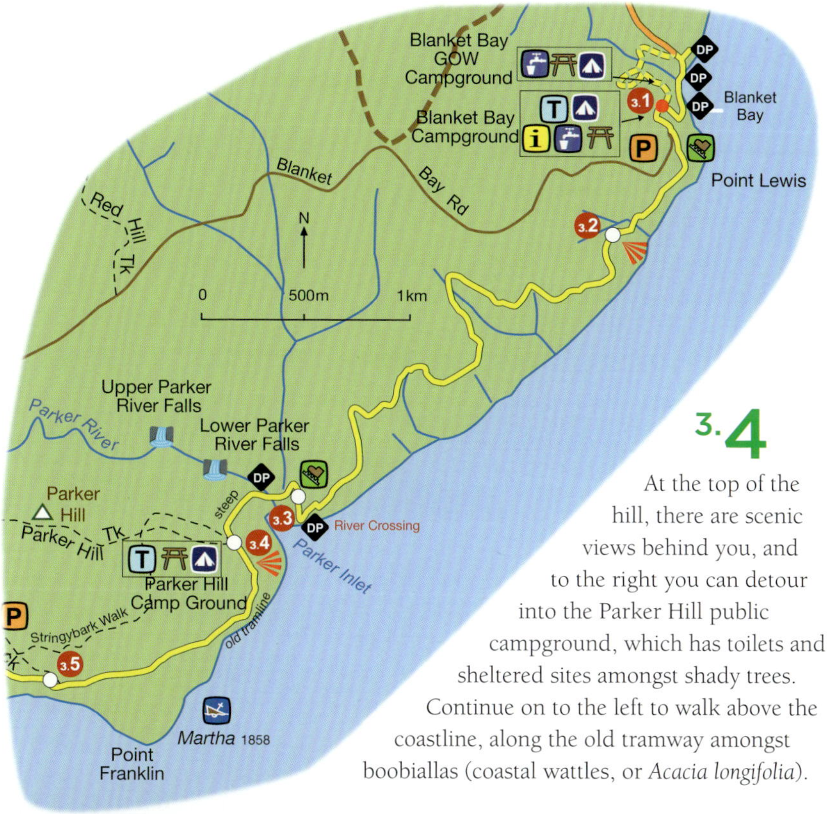

3.4

At the top of the hill, there are scenic views behind you, and to the right you can detour into the Parker Hill public campground, which has toilets and sheltered sites amongst shady trees. Continue on to the left to walk above the coastline, along the old tramway amongst boobiallas (coastal wattles, or *Acacia longifolia*).

Parker Inlet - the Hunt for Eric the Red

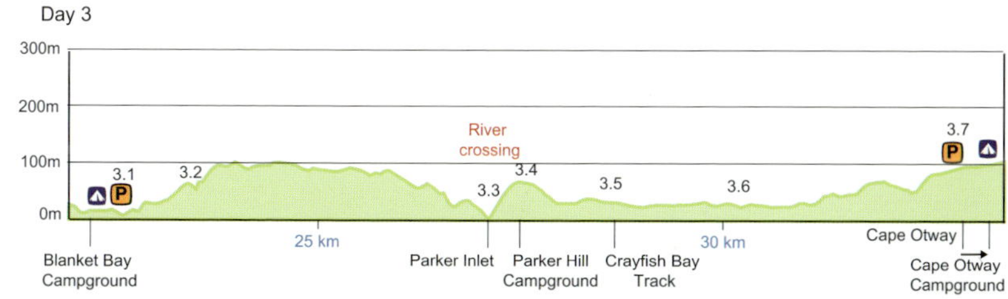

Day 3 Blanket Bay to Cape Otway

Boardwalk over fragile dunes

3.5 The track opens out at a wide track junction. Continue straight ahead (signed *GOW and towards Crayfish Bay*) or take the 100-metre-long sidetrack down to the wide sandy beach at Point Franklin, looking out for *Eric The Red's* anchor embedded in the rocks. You can choose to continue along the beach here at low tide, around Seal Point, to Crayfish Bay – at the end of the little beach there are some steep wooden stairs back up to rejoin the GOW. If you have stayed up on the GOW track instead of going down on the beach, watch carefully for GOW signage here as there are multiple path crossings. The GOW takes a sharp turn to the left, signed *towards Crayfish Bay* (630 metres), where you can again opt to go down to the beach.

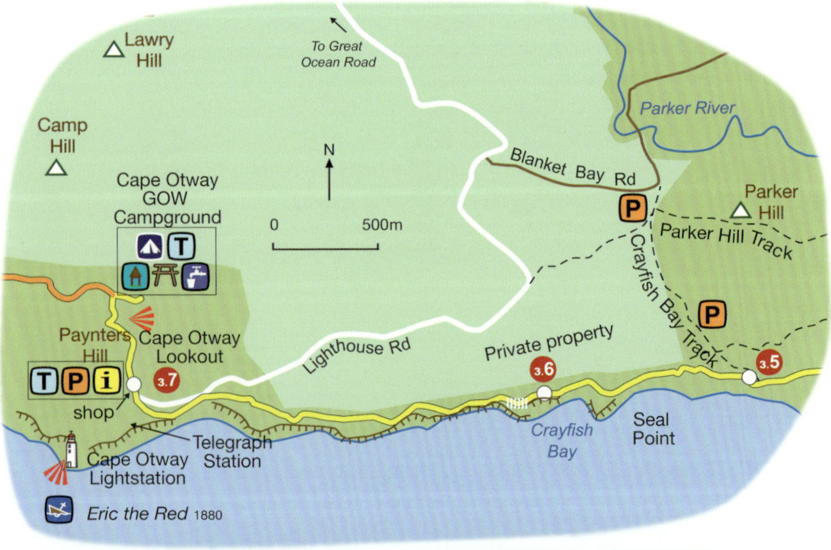

3.6 From the GOW main track above the western end of Crayfish Bay, the path follows the contours of the sand dunes – there is no shade on this section. Wooden stairs and board walks keep you off vulnerable sections of the dunes which contain Aboriginal middens and sections of petrified forest, as you start to catch glimpses of Cape Otway Lightstation in the distance.

Steps down to Crayfish Bay

3.7a DAY WALKERS arrive into the car park at Cape Otway Lightstation, where you can pay to gain access and enjoy a coffee and scone if the café is open (check before planning on it!) before getting your lift for the day.

3.7b CAMPERS, continue through the car park towards the GOW Campground a short distance along the GOW track past the lightstation complex. Official GOW campers get free access to the lightstation as part of their Parks Vic bookings.

First view of Cape Otway Lightstation

Alternate routes

Parks Victoria recommends use of only the ***GOW inland*** route options where options are available. Alternate routes along the beaches and rock platforms are officially signed, but can potentially be quite dangerous. Where it is quite unwise, regardless of tides, even for experienced and highly capable walkers, we have indicated 'not recommended'. Decision Point numbering/naming aligns with the official map/signage.

GOW Official Decision Point	Description/location	Conditions	Exit/escape options
Blanket Bay Decision Point **6A**	Blanket Bay Beach on the southside of Blanket Bay Creek.	Easy short walk along the beach past the boat ramp.	Easy.
Blanket Bay Decision Point **6B**	Blanket Bay to Parker River via rock platforms.	Extended rock platforms and deep gullies. Requires scrambling. Impassable on rising tides.	*Seriously* not recommended. No exit points before Parker Inlet.
Parker Inlet Decision Point **7**	Parker Inlet - unbridged river crossing.	At low tide this is a straightforward walk across the sand and a trickle of water. When the tide and waves are rolling in, this can quickly become neck-deep, dangerous and impassable.	**No inland option.** Should not be attempted at high or incoming tides. You will need to wait until the water recedes and it is safe to cross.
Parker Inlet Decision Point **7A**	End of beach over Parker River, coastline via Point Franklin to Crayfish Bay.	2 km of rock platforms, deep gullies, covered by tides, freak waves, poor sight lines, scrambling required.	Not recommended. Extremely limited exit/ escape options.

Parker Inlet

Coastal Banksia

The Shipwreck of *Eric the Red* (1880)

Some remnants of *Eric the Red* can sometimes be seen at low tide embedded in the flat beach near the mouth of the Parker River – look carefully, as you may mistake the wood remnants for flat black rocks, and depending on the shifting sands, you may not see them at all. The ship was named for the first European to establish a settlement on Greenland (around 980 A.D), Icelandic Viking Eric 'the Red-Haired' Thorvaldsson. The American-owned ship carried coal between Britain and America in the 1870s, then bat poo (guano) and nitrates from South America. When it was wrecked in 1880, it had been chartered to bring American cargo to Melbourne, including exhibits for the International Exhibition. After 85 days at sea, the ship approached Cape Otway and was steering by the lightstation just after midnight before striking the Otway Reef a number of times, with heavy seas causing the ship to break up entirely in a mere twelve minutes. Captain Jacques Allen gave a harrowing first person insight to the shipwreck.

(The Argus newspaper 14/9/1880):

"The mizzen top mast fell with all the rigging, but strange to say, not a man was hurt by it, although they were all standing about. As soon as I found out there was no hope I said to Ned Sewell, the owner's son, and the third mate on board "Stick to me, and hang on to this mizzen mast". I peeled off everything I had on except my drawers thinking I would be able to swim better without my clothes; and Sewell and myself, clinging to the mast, were washed overboard.... It was a fearful sea; I have never seen anything like it. Just as I left the spar my drawers got down my legs, and entangled them, and down I went. I managed to clear one of my legs and on coming up I managed to get hold of some floating timber. There was a clear space of water between this timber and the deck, with the exception of the spare royal yard, and I again started, but the surf struck me and I went over and over. I managed to get hold of the spare yard, and after holding on to it for some time I managed to get to the deck. When I was pulled on to it I could not move, being so numb and cramped with the cold. The men had some blankets and other things which they had got from the passengers' room in the deckhouse, and they wrapped me in these. Shortly after I got onto the wreck we made out the steamer's lights, and as soon as she was within hearing distance the men halloed. This must have been about half-past four...... and at daylight they picked us up off the wreck. We had drifted about four miles from the reef where the ship struck.... All those who were rescued were more or less bruised. One man had two or three ribs broken, and another had some fingers crushed off. My left foot is very much hurt, and I am black and blue from head to foot. I never knew such a ten minutes as that of the wreck, and I thought the time had come for me to 'hand in my checks'".

WRECK OF THE SHIP ERIC THE RED, CAPE OTWAY: RESCUE OF THE CREW BY THE DAWN.

Three of the crew and one of the two passengers drowned. One body was found washed up at Cape Otway and is buried in the lightstation cemetery. Wreckage and cargo washed up all over the Victorian coast, and particularly at Point Franklin, where one of the anchors is still in the rocks (photo page 49). Another anchor is on display at Cape Otway Lightstation, and still other salvaged remnants can be seen at the Apollo Bay Museum.

Cape Otway Lightstation

A lightstation at Cape Otway was considered essential in the 19th Century, given the dangers of Bass Strait and that the growth and defence of the new colony depended on safe shipping of labour and supplies. The 26,000-kilometre route from Europe followed Australia's southern coast and it was the last few days' sailing which presented a major navigational threat. As the Southern Ocean pushes through the comparatively shallow 84-kilometre gap between King Island and Cape Otway, it produces huge swells and treacherous conditions, especially for sailing ships. Celestial navigation provided limited accuracy of a ship's position, made worse by chart errors, miscalculations and bad weather. Consequently, the western entry to Bass Strait became known as *'Threading the Eye of the Needle'*. Captains followed the coast to provide certainty but without definitive beacons there were numerous shipwrecks. In 1845, 400 people died after the emigrant barque *Cataraqui* sank off King Island. This event remains Australia's largest civilian maritime disaster and became the catalyst for the construction of the lightstation at Cape Otway. A huge undertaking given the area's remoteness, it took Charles La Trobe three attempts to even reach the Cape. It was built between 1846-48 using sandstone quarried at Parker River. Remarkably no cement was used.

Working life at the lighthouse was physically hard. Keepers worked a 4-hour watch, refilling the lamps with sperm whale oil, clearing soot and winding the mechanism. The lightstation burned almost 400 litres of oil monthly which was carried up 78 steps to the lantern room. When the fuel changed to kerosene in 1891, 15-litre tins needed to be lugged up nightly. The harsh marine environment required buildings and grounds to be well maintained and work increased with the arrival of the telegraph line in 1859, which often failed due to fires and falling trees. Given its remoteness, the keepers and their families made the Cape Otway Lightstation a small village: it even had its own school between 1881 and 1933 and its small cemetery is quite poignant. The community needed to be almost entirely self-sufficient, with vegetable gardens, orchards, chickens, pigs, even a small dairy herd, as the lack of road access meant resupply was by boat just a couple of times a year. Supplies were landed at Blanket Bay (where the ruins of the old lighthouse storage shed are still visible), then hauled up the hill onto a tramway. In the early 20th century, goods came every 3 months by narrow-gauge railway to Lavers Hill, then were transported to the Cape by cart over 1-3 days. By the mid- 1930s, the track to Colac eventually became passable by motor vehicles.

Cape Otway's strategic position also made it militarily important. In WWI, the lightstation was used by the Australian Navy as a Lookout Station and in WWII it became a Naval War Signal Station. In 1942 a radar bunker was built to monitor enemy submarines after the first US ship to sink in WWII, the SS City of Raville, struck a German mine 14 kilometres south of the Cape. The radar station was discontinued in 1946 but the bunker has been restored.

Having operated continuously since 1848, the light was finally decommissioned in January 1994, making it the longest continuously operating lighthouse on the Australian mainland. It was replaced by a low powered solar light in front of the original tower. Given this wonderful maritime and defence history, it is well worth spending some time exploring the lightstation and its associated buildings and graveyard.

Rainbow Falls

Day 4 Cape Otway to Aire River

At a glance

Distance: 9.5 km (camping), 9.9 km (day walk)

Time: approx. 3.5 hours

Difficulty: Medium

Highlights: Historic lightstation and cemetery, Rainbow Falls, beach walking

A couple of detours on the Walk to Aire River from Cape Otway are well worth the extra distance. Just a short way off the main track, the Cape Otway Cemetery is a sad reminder of the harsh conditions and isolation experienced by the lighthouse keepers and their families and of the treacherous coast which wrecked many a ship. A little further off the track and along the beach, dependent on tides, is Rainbow Falls, fed by a spring which seeps through mosses and algae before trickling down the cliffs; the colours are subtle and depend on the time of day and amount of sunshine. The Walk is quite exposed for most of the day and finishes at the now peaceful Aire River, which belies its role in the region's tragic history.

Through the Tea-Tree tunnel, leaving Cape Otway.

Day 4 Cape Otway to Aire River

	Start	Finish	
Camping option	Cape Otway GOW Campground, Waypoint 4.2	Aire River GOW Campground	9.5 km
Day walk option	Cape Otway Lightstation car park	Aire River Day Visitor's Shelter	9.9 km

Walk directions

4.1 FOR DAY WALKERS, walk to the end of the lightstation car park to the information board and around the gate. Follow the sign to the *Cape Otway GOW campground and Lighthouse Lookout* and keep a lookout for the gap on the left which allows for a view back to the lightstation.

4.2 Back on the GOW, at the bottom of the track turn right to follow the yellow GOW trail marker. Walk past the path to the right which leads to the GOW campground and continue in the direction of Aire Valley GOW Campground. FOR CAMPERS, start the day by returning to the main track and turn right.

The sandy track winds through coastal tea-tree tunnels, white bearded heath, and she-oaks.

Cape Otway Cemetery

Station Beach

4.3 At the track junction, continue straight ahead, ignoring the *Bracks Access and Bimbi Park* signs to the right. Just past the GOW sign, take the small track to the right to find the Cape Otway cemetery. Retrace your steps back to the main path and turn right. Eventually the track reaches the top of the cliffs, affording views to the rocks below. It continues hugging the cliffs for a short distance before heading inland and then returning to wind along sand dunes.

4.4 Continue straight at the GOW directions board, signed *Aire River via Cliff Top 5.5 km*, to follow the GOW path, ignoring the sidetrack to Bimbi Park. There is also the option here to walk to Aire River via Station Beach (at low tide): turn left to walk down the boardwalk to the beach, then right along the beach, bearing in mind that it's 4 kilometres on very soft sand. (To visit Rainbow Falls, see the breakout box on page 66). The main GOW track meanders above the surf, through dunes and wind-pruned coastal vegetation, eventually coming out on a rocky platform with expansive views along the coast to the west.

4.5 You will reach a post with the yellow GOW trail marker (**Decision Point 8A**). If you don't want to take the beachwalk option to Aire River, continue along the main GOW inland track which winds through the dunes.

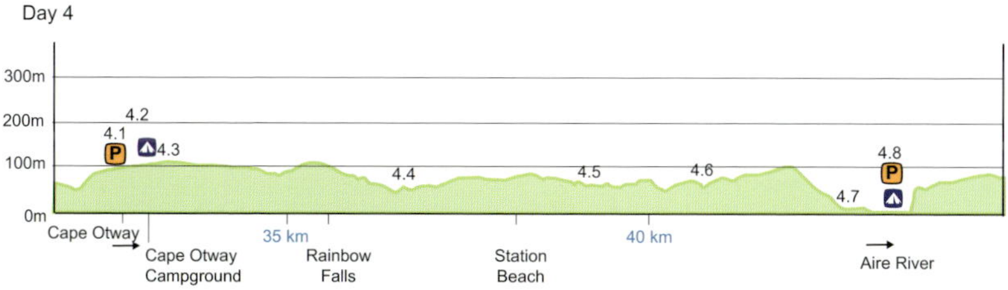

Day 4 Cape Otway to Aire River

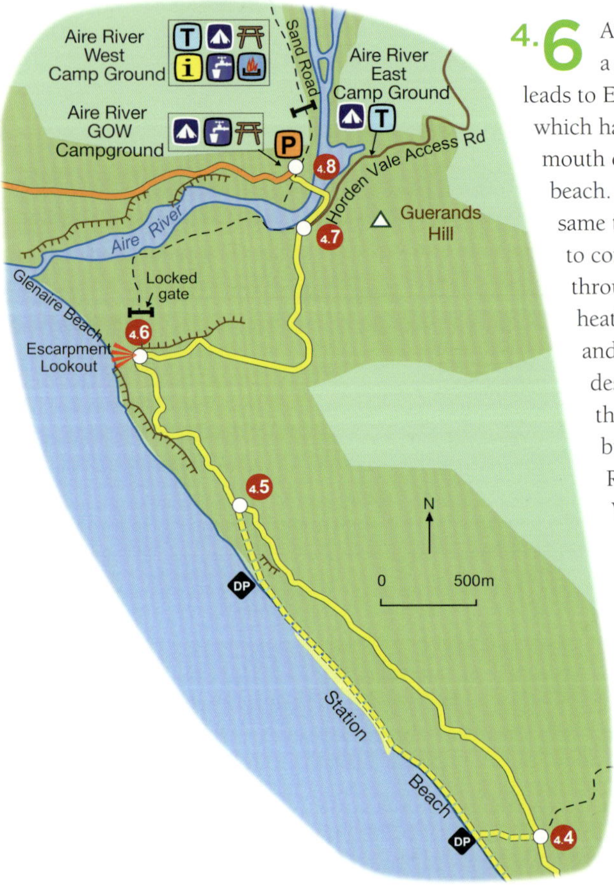

4.6 At the next trail marker, a short path to the left leads to Escarpment Lookout which has views down to the mouth of the Aire River and beach. Return along the same track and turn left to continue to Aire River through bracken, bearded heath, draped sea spinach and rhogodia. As you descend the sandy path, there are views of the bridge across the Aire River and up the Aire Valley.

4.7 Where the path meets the 4WD track, turn right and walk beside the river towards the bridge (turning left takes you to Glenaire Beach). Cross the bridge and continue straight ahead.

Glenaire Beach Escarpment lookout

Aire River

4.8 FOR DAY WALKERS, the pick-up is from the Day Visitor's Shelter near the Aire River West Campground. FOR CAMPERS, take the path behind the Day Visitor's Shelter and car park, past the toilet block on the right and zig zag up the hill, to the GOW campground.

Steps to Aire River GOW campground

No shade on the track above Station Beach

Return detour to Rainbow Falls

Optional detour to Rainbow Falls at low tide

If the tide is low and the sun is out, the 3-kilometre return detour along the beach to Rainbow Falls is very worth your while. At Waypoint 4.4, turn left to walk down the narrow boardwalk. When you reach the end of the boardwalk continue straight ahead past the GOW sign to your left (don't be tempted to turn left before the beach as the sign indicates, as you'll end up struggling through undergrowth and trampling the fragile dunes) and up and over the dunes to the beach and **Decision Point 8**. Turn left to walk along the sand towards the rocky headland. Step up onto the rock platform and around the point to catch the first glimpse of the Falls and then continue on to get a closer look at the rock face and its very colourful algae. Return to **Decision Point 8** and retrace your steps back up to the GOW then turn left to rejoin the GOW. Alternatively, if the tide is favourable you can build your calf muscles and walk west a further 2 kilometres along Station Beach to **Decision Point 8A** just before Aire River, where you can regain the GOW track.

Blanket Bay Massacre

Tragically, there is a dark history of clashes between Traditional Owners and settlers in this beautiful region. The areas around Blanket Bay and Aire River were once the scene of a brutal massacre. In 1846 surveyor George Smythe was sent by Governor Latrobe to conduct a survey of the coast around the Otway Ranges. He set up camp at Blanket Bay. Leaving a few men behind, he continued his exploration west towards Aire River. On his return he discovered that one of his men, James Conroy, was dead. It is believed that Conroy had abducted a Gadubanud woman and was killed in retaliation. Smythe returned to Melbourne to inform Latrobe of the death and while there he organised an expedition to avenge Conroy's death. The party tracked down a group of the Gadubanud camped on the bank of the Aire River estuary and attacked them, murdering between eight to twenty men, women and children.

Aire River

Alternate routes

Parks Victoria *recommends the use of only the* ***GOW inland*** *route options where these options are available*. Alternate routes along the beaches and rock platforms can be interesting but should only be attempted at low tide (preferably outgoing) in calm weather and may involve exposure to dangerous (including freak) waves, currents, tides, rock scrambling, gullies, poor sightlines and limited or no escape options. Where it is quite unwise, regardless of tides, even for experienced and highly capable walkers, we have listed as 'not recommended'. Decision Point numbering aligns with the official map and signage.

GOW Official Decision Point	Description/location	Conditions	Exit/escape options
Station Beach Decision Point **8**	Station Beach to Rainbow Falls Detour.	3 km return slog along soft sandy beach and rock platforms. Passable at low tide only.	May need to wait for water to recede if you wish to see the Falls.
Station Beach Decision Point **8**	Station Beach west towards Aire River.	2 km soft sandy beach which is regularly covered by rising tides and large waves.	Possible to clamber up dunes and off the beach at points and at **8A** if necessary.
Station Beach Decision Point **8A**	From west end of Station Beach to Aire River.	1.5 km of beach and rock platforms regularly covered by large waves and high tides.	**Not recommended.** No exit options before Glenaire Beach/Aire River.

Johanna GOW campground

Day 5 Aire Valley to Johanna Beach

At a glance

Distance: 13.6 km (camping), 13.2 km (day walk)

Time: approx. 4.5 hours

Difficulty: Medium

Highlights: Grass-tree forests, Castle Cove underslip, unbridged Johanna River crossing

There are some opportunities along this section, when the path nears the coast, for spectacular views back along the way you've come and forward to where you're going. Along the stretch between Aire River and Castle Cove lookout for flame robins that are often seen leading you along the path. The day concludes at Johanna Beach, named after the schooner *Joanna* which was wrecked at the mouth of the Johanna River in September 1843. The beach is noted for its powerful surf and has sometimes been used as an alternative to Bell's Beach for surfing competitions when the waves have been too small there. The unbridged river crossing can be dangerous except at low tide, so check your timings before setting out, or you may have to be prepared to sit and wait for the tide to recede.

Crossing Johanna River

Day 5 Aire Valley to Johanna Beach

	Start	Finish	
Camping option	Aire Valley GOW Campground, Waypoint 5.2	Johanna Beach GOW campground	13.6 km
Day walk option	Aire River Day Visitor's car park	Johanna Beach car park	13.2 km

Walk directions

5.1 FOR DAY WALKERS, follow the yellow gravel path behind the Day Visitor's Shelter in the Aire River car park to walk past the toilet block on your right towards the Aire River GOW Campground. If you are lucky, you may spot some koalas in the manna gums near the Day Visitor's Shelter area.

5.2 At the top of the hill, turn left to walk past the Aire River GOW Camp shelter, towards Castle Cove and Johanna Beach Campground. FOR CAMPERS, rejoin the GOW track. As the path rises, take the opportunity to look back over the estuary and up the Aire Valley. Where the path winds closer to the cliffs, pause at the lookout above Sentinel Rock for expansive views. The 70 metres between Sentinel Rock and west to Eagle Rock is the site of an ancient rockfall. The track continues along the cliff top then descends to wander below the vegetated cliff face, providing an entirely different perspective.

5.3 After stepping over the low barrier, follow the path around to the right and then to the left, following the yellow GOW marker. For a short but strenuous detour, the sandy path to the left leads steeply down to Castle Cove beach, a great place for a snack or lunch.

5.4 The GOW path travels beside the road for a short distance. At the information board, turn left up to Castle Cove lookout. Retrace your steps down towards the road and turn left to continue along the GOW. The path turns

Towards Castle Cove

Day 5 Aire Valley to Johanna Beach

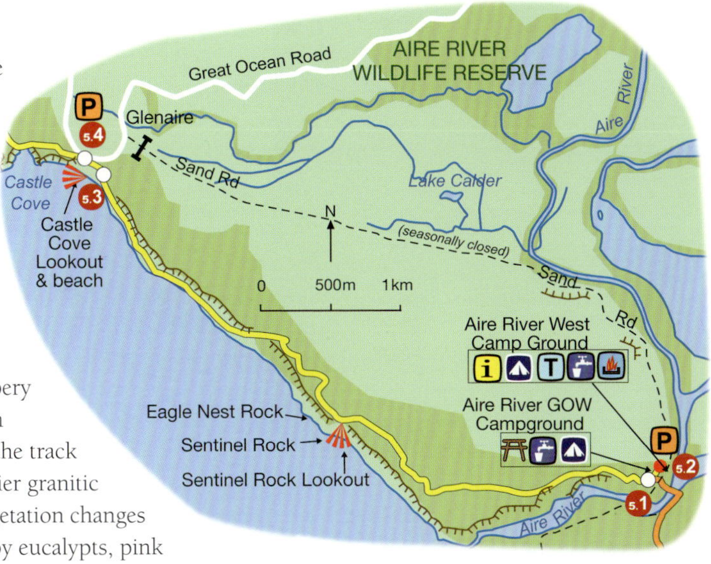

away from the road and meanders up and down the hills and through coastal scrub. Take care if wet, as it can be slippery and muddy in parts, before the track changes to drier granitic sand. The vegetation changes too, to scrubby eucalypts, pink and white heath, grass trees, callistemons and banksias. At the lookout seat, enjoy the views back towards Castle Cove and glimpses of the Aire Valley to the west. The path from the lookout winds through a valley where the trees arch across the track and the Walk crosses gullies and footbridges. The track then zigzags gently up and through an avenue of grass trees and past strategically placed seats. After the boot cleaning station, as you move along the narrow boardwalk,the track returns to coastal scrub.

Remember to look back occasionally!

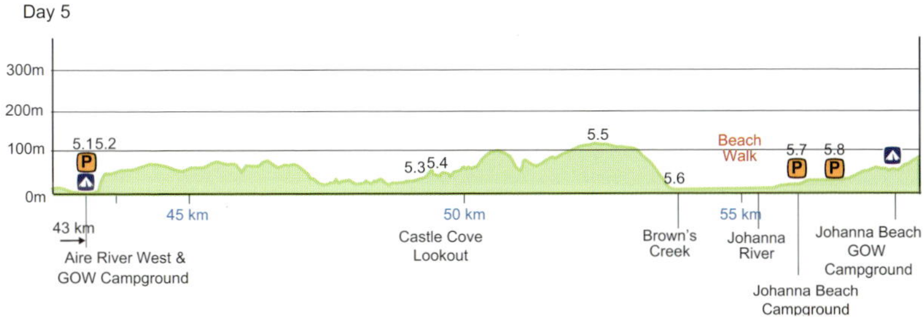

Day 5 Aire Valley to Johanna Beach

Through the grass trees

5.5 From the next boot cleaning station, the track passes through an incredibly dense grasstree forest. These plants are particularly susceptible to the cinnamon fungus which has devastated large areas of native bushland. The track descends steeply down to the beach and Brown Creek, usually a dry river bed.

5.6 When you reach the beach and the sign for Decision Point 9, turn right to begin the 2-kilometre walk along the soft sand of Johanna Beach. There is no inland alternative for this section of the walk so please be aware of tides and conditions. At the Johanna River mouth you will most likely need to take off your boots to wade across. Depending on tides, ocean swell and rainfall, this can be a dangerous crossing, so plan your walk to cross at low/outgoing tide. You may otherwise need to wait for the water to recede.

Just past Castle Cove

5.7 As you continue along the beach on the other side of the river, shortly before the rocky outcrop, there is a GOW marker up on the dune to the right: Decision Point 9A. You can either rejoin the GOW inland path here for a break from the sand walking or continue along the beach for another 500 metres to Decision Point 9B, which is unmarked, before rejoining the GOW at the car park. On the inland GOW track, walk up the path and just to the left is the Lower Lookout for views back along Johanna Beach. The track straight ahead takes you to the Upper Lookout which gives views both east and west. Continue along the path as it curves to the right, following the direction of the blue arrow. At the car park, walk along the Old Coach Road as it curves to the left through the drive-in campground and then winds its way beside paddocks and farmland. This is a shared road so beware of cars. There are GOW markers to help you find your way through. Continue past the toilet block and information board on the left, over the grass towards the GOW marker.

Entering Johanna Beach

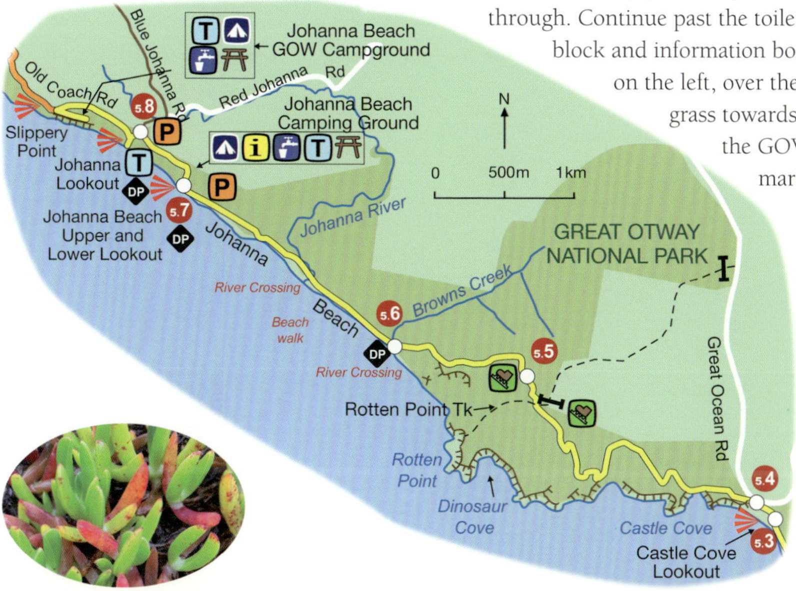

The *Joanna*

Forming part of the *Shipwreck Coast*, Johanna Beach has a reputation for powerful, wild surf and, due to the beach facing west, it catches the big swells. Along the 130-kilometre stretch of coast from Cape Otway to Port Fairy, 638 ships have been wrecked but only about 240 of them have ever been found. One of these ships, the schooner *Joanna*, on its maiden voyage from Launceston to Port Fairy, hit some rough weather causing it to leak badly. On the 22nd of September 1843 it was washed ashore and wrecked near the mouth of the river (now known as Johanna River) and a crew member was swept overboard and lost. The survivors embarked on a 7-day journey to reach Geelong and are thought to be the first Europeans to have set foot on this part of the coast.

5.8 **FOR DAY WALKERS**, the pick-up is from the Johanna Beach car park. **FOR CAMPERS**, from the car park veer right up the hill with the ocean and beach down to your left. At the break in the fence, turn right up the grassy path signed to *Johanna Beach GOW Campground and Milanesia Beach 10 km*. Keep following the mowed path as it arcs to the right, ignoring the smaller path which goes straight. Climb the hill beneath a canopy of she-oaks and manna gums. Turn left at the T-junction to get to the Johanna GOW Campground. This camp is away from the Johanna Beach crowds, has panoramic views back along the coast and a mighty fine view from the loo as well.

Grass trees and *Phytophthora cinnamomi* (Cinnamon Fungus)

This section of the Walk goes through a lovely section of grass tree forest. There are 16 different species of grass trees (*Xanthorrhoea*) in Australia. The long thin fronds and irregular, fire-blackened trunks can sometimes represent plants more than 400 years old. They are some of our slowest-growing (1-6 cm per year) and most resilient plants, living in very nutrient-poor soils and responding after bushfires with profuse, towering flower spikes. However, they are also very susceptible to *Phytophera cinnamomi*, a horrible introduced water-borne mould which attacks the roots of plants, most visibly our iconic grass trees. It causes root-rot, severe dieback and death. While many of the grasstrees on the walk are still in good condition, you may see some along the way which are brown and looking like they are 'crumbling away'- most probably suffering dieback from this fungus. The boot hygiene stations are in place at various points along the GOW in order to help minimise the risks of it spreading between sectors. Please clean your boots thoroughly before and after the GOW, and use every boot cleaning station along the way enthusiastically, really kicking into the brushes to remove soil and 'dipping' on the metal plates to ensure the soles and sides of your boot are doused in the disinfectant.

Johanna Beach

Alternate routes

Parks Victoria recommends the use of only the ***GOW inland*** route options where these options are available. Alternate routes along the beaches and rock platforms can be interesting but should only be attempted at low tide (preferably outgoing) in calm weather and may involve exposure to dangerous (including freak) waves, currents, tides, rock scrambling, gullies, poor sightlines and limited or no escape options. Where it is quite unwise, regardless of tides, even for experienced and highly capable walkers, we have listed as 'not recommended'. Decision Point names/numbering aligns with the official map and signage.

GOW Official Decision Point	Description/location	Conditions	Exit/escape options
Johanna Beach Decision Point **9**	Where the track meets Johanna Beach at Browns Creek.	Soft sand beach walking and river crossing. Check tide times.	No alternate inland option. May need to wait for waters to recede. No exit for 2 km.
Johanna Beach Decision Point **9A**	West end of Johanna Beach at the car park.	Soft sand beach. Possible at low tide and in calm conditions.	No exit for 500 m. Take inland track, via signed path to Upper and Lower lookouts and public campground.
Johanna Beach Decision Point **9B**	Johanna Beach, western end of beach before rocky outcrop towards Milanesia Beach.	No coast access to Milanesia Beach, rock platforms, deep gutters and beaches are impassable owing to high tides, waves and cliffs.	Not recommended. No escape routes.

Lion Headland from Milanesia Beach

Day 6 Johanna Beach to Ryans Den

At a glance

Distance: 13.6 km (camping), 14.3 km (day walk)

Time: 4-5 hours

Difficulty: Medium – lots of stairs, ups and downs, very slippery when wet

Highlights: Quirky roadside stall, Milanesia Beach, Lion Headland, kangaroos

While the first part of this section of the Walk is along an inland shared track (listed for future re-alignment), where there are often large mobs of kangaroos grazing alongside the cattle, it is all worth it to access stunning, remote Milanesia Beach and the views back to Lion Headland. In winter and wet weather, the clay-surfaces of the descents can be very slippery, as the skid marks of walkers ahead of you will attest, so hiking poles can really come into their own. There are many stairs, quite architectural in places, though also very slippery when wet. The rest of the day takes you through a variety of coastal vegetation, set just back from towering sea cliffs, and wild and inaccessible coastlines below, with the sound of crashing waves a constant reminder of the power of the Southern Ocean. Ryans Den Campground is another of the really special secluded hike-in/out campgrounds the GOW has to offer. For day walkers, it's worth noting that the pick-up point, where the Ryans Den Track connects with the Great Ocean Road between Yuulong and Wattle Hill, is small and unmarked with extremely limited parking. It is also in an area with limited mobile reception and is on a windy section of the Great Ocean Road, so ensure your arrangements are clear (GPS S38 747 084, E143 279 052).

Lots of ups and downs today

Day 6 Johanna Beach to Ryans Den

	Start	Finish	
Camping option	Johanna Beach GOW Campground	Ryans Den GOW Campground	13.6 km
Day walk option	Johanna Beach car park	Ryans Den Track/GOR	14.3 km

Old private cottage on Milanesia Runnng Creek

Walk directions

6.1 FOR DAY WALKERS, from the Johanna Beach car park veer right up the hill past the Johanna Lookout, with the ocean and beach down to your left. At the break in the fence, turn right up the grassy path signed to *Johanna Beach GOW campground and Milanesia Beach 10 km.*

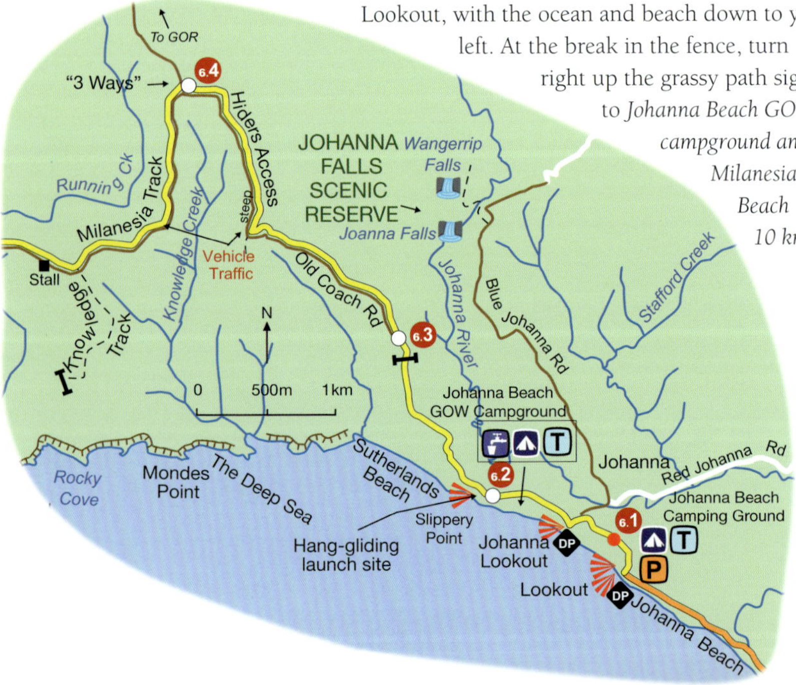

Keep following the mowed path as it arcs to the right, ignoring the smaller path which goes straight. Climb the hill beneath a canopy of she-oaks and manna gums and turn right at the T-junction (turning left will take you to the loo and picnic table in the Johanna Beach GOW campground). **FOR CAMPERS**, from the Johanna Beach GOW campground, walk back down to the GOW and continue straight ahead.

6.2 The open area you walk past after leaving the campground, is the Johanna Hang Gliding and Paragliding launch site, so don't be too concerned if someone with wings attached is seemingly jumping off the cliff. For those without wings, the path follows a GOW marker arrow, with views over the valley and Johanna River. Ignore the gate confusingly marked *'Management vehicles and walkers only'* and continue along the grassy track which winds around the hill.

6.3 At the next gate, join the shared gravel vehicle track (Old Coach Road/ Hiders Access). The Old Coach Road was the main access road before the construction of the Great Ocean Road. Watch out for cars as you make your way steadily uphill through mixed eucalypts and tree ferns, following the ridgeline past farms.

6.4 At the road junction (*'3 Ways'*) at the top of the hill (the road sign: *'drivers beware'* also should apply to hikers), turn left, signed *Milanesia Track* and continue down the vehicle road, past plantation forests on the right. After 2 kilometres, ignoring *Knowledge Track* on the left, continue ahead to pass some private properties including one that generously hosts a whacky sea captain water point for hikers!

Hikers Friend water point

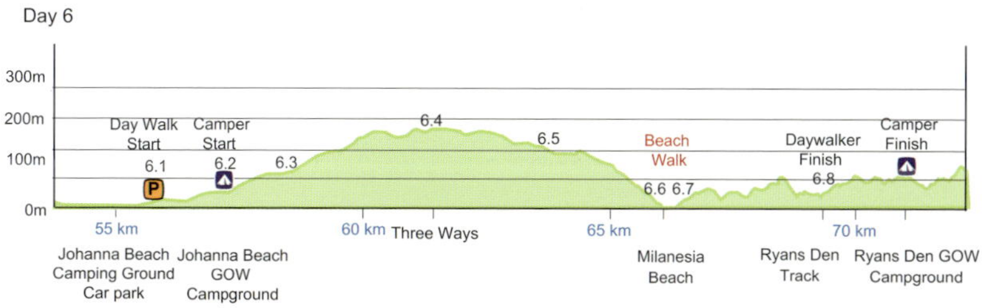

Day 6 Johanna Beach to Ryans Den

Slippery when wet

6.5 The gravel road enters the forest and the GOW continues past a locked steel gate along the Milanesia Track for some time, then steeply (and slippily if wet!) down to Milanesia Beach. Hiking poles are a great help in this section.

6.6 Just before you cross Milanesia Creek, look back along the creek to the right for the surprising and picturesque white cottage upstream, which was built long before the National Park was declared and remains in private hands (the road you have just slid/walked down is part of a shared access track). Continue over the stepping stones and onto Milanesia Beach, ideally at low tide as there is no inland route for the next 300 metres. Milanesia Beach was named for the ship of the same name which was stranded here for a number of days in 1902. Make sure you look back as you walk along this remote beach for the awe-inspiring view of Lion Headland behind you.

Across Milanesia Creek

High tide seaweed as you exit Milanesia Beach

Day 6 Johanna Beach to Ryans Den

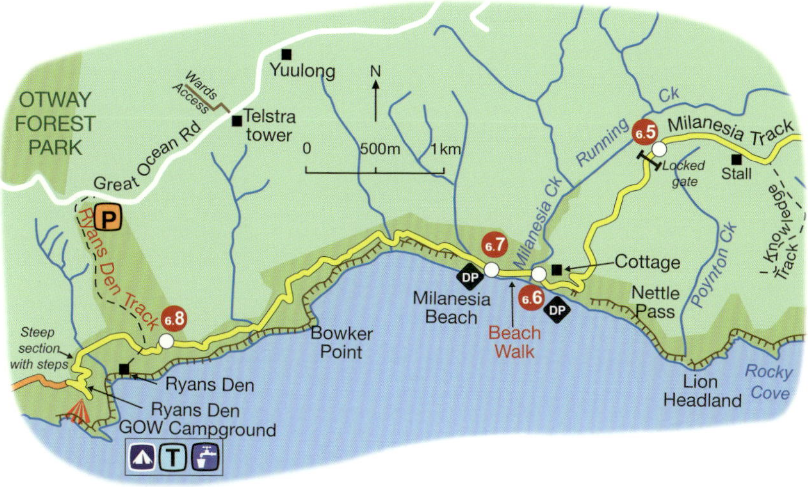

Slogging up from Milanesia Beach

6.7 At the end of the beach, head steeply up the hill then up via more gentle switchbacks and down the other side via slippery-if-wet stairs through coastal tea-tree. You'll eventually reach the top of Bowker Point and, on a clear day, can look back all the way to the Cape Otway Lightstation to impress yourself with how far you have walked! From here you will head down some more steep stairs and through the mixed coastal shrubs high above the ocean.

Today is step day

Day 6 Johanna Beach to Ryans Den

6.8 **FOR DAY WALKERS**, keep an eye out for the GOW25 trackmarker, signed *Great Ocean Road 1km*. Turn right here to walk up the path which becomes *Ryans Den Track*, to the junction with the Great Ocean Road for your pick up/car shuttle. **FOR CAMPERS**, ignore the turn off and continue straight ahead, ascending yet more stairs, to reach Ryans Den GOW Campground.

Turnoff to Ryans Den Track

An early GOW hiker: Charles La Trobe (1801-1875)

The Otways in La Trobe's day

Museum of Victoria collection

Port Phillip District Superintendent, Charles Joseph La Trobe, was ordered by the NSW colony's Governor Gipps, to "find a practical route" to Cape Otway in order to make preparations to build a lighthouse. It was considered a priority in order to prevent the continuing losses and tragedies of lives and ships along what is still known as The Shipwreck Coast. The clamour for action from the House of Commons in the UK came to a head after the devastating loss of 400 lives aboard the *Cataraqui* in 1845, off the coast of King Island. How could the colony be built if there was no labour arriving safely? La Trobe was suited to the task: apart from his more notable contributions to the young colony — establishing Melbourne University and what was to become the State Library — La Trobe was a dedicated hiker and explorer. He and his Swiss wife had explored the Swiss and Italian Alps and in 1833, he had walked and ridden a horse from the east to the west coast of America and ventured further afield to Mexico and the West Indies. Despite his experience and enthusiasm, La Trobe tried a number of times but was defeated by the dense bush and sea cliffs of the Otways. In 1846 he described the bush-bashing between Cape Volney and Milanesia in particular, as *"the most arduous day of severe exertion I have ever encountered"*. Even with a local coastal Traditional Owner and pastoralist as guides, it took five attempts over three months before he eventually succeeded. Some of the route on this section retraces the original surveyed path, which was to become The Old Coach Road.

Milanesia Beach

Alternate routes

Parks Victoria *recommends the use of only the **GOW inland** route options where these options are available*. Alternate routes along the beaches and rock platforms are officially signed, but can potentially be quite dangerous. Where it is quite unwise, regardless of tides, even for experienced and highly capable walkers, we have indicated 'not recommended'. Decision Point numbering/naming aligns with the official map/signage.

GOW Official Decision Point	Description/location	Conditions	Exit/escape options
Milanesia Beach Decision Point **10**	Beachwalk of 300m from Milanesia Creek (unbridged but with stepping stones).	Stepping stones over creek mouth. Soft sand on beach – aim to cross at low or on an outgoing tide. Watch for waves.	No alternate inland route exists. You may need to wait for tide to recede if impassable.
Milanesia Beach Decision Point **10A**	Western End of Milanesia Beach.	750m of rock platforms, scrambling, deep gullies, high sea cliffs, poor sightlines, often impassable.	Not recommended. No exit routes.

Cape Volney and Point Reginald from Ryans Den

Looking back from Cape Volney

Day 7 Ryans Den to Devils Kitchen/Wreck Beach

This section is often considered one of the wildest and more challenging sections of the track and is a favourite of many for that reason. There is a lot of variety and of course many ups and downs. For fungi lovers doing the walk in autumn or winter, there is a particularly rich sheltered bush section (Waypoint 7.5) which can be a bit of a wonderland. This day of the GOW also holds many stories and evidence of the Otway Coast's tragic shipwrecks. The opportunity to explore the shipwreck remnants and old anchors of the *Fiji* and the *Gabrielle* on Wreck beach are not to be missed, so try and time your walk to ensure low tide either at the end of the day, or start of the following day, as the anchors and beach are entirely inaccessible at high tide.

At a glance

Distance: 13.4 km (camping), 12.4 km (day walk)

Time: 5 hours

Difficulty: Hard, up and downs, very slippery when wet

Highlights: Views, ups and downs, fungi in winter, Moonlight Head, Wreck Beach anchors

Moonlight Head Cemetery sundial

Fiji anchor on Wreck Beach

Day 7 Ryans Den to Devils Kitchen/Wreck Beach

	Start	Finish	
Camping option	Ryans Den GOW Campground	Devils Kitchen GOW Campground	13.4 km
Day walk option	Ryans Den Track/GOR	Wreck Beach car park	12.4 km

Walk directions

7.1 FOR DAY WALKERS, from the access to *Ryans Den Track* on the Great Ocean Road (refer notes for Day 6: easy to miss; on the left/south-west of the Telstra Tower after Yuulong; limited parking for only 2 vehicles), walk down the locked vehicle management track until you reach the vehicle turnaround. The walking track continues off to the right and downhill towards the coast. Turn right at the GOW track crossroads to rejoin the GOW. Get ready for a lot of very steep stairs. At the top of the hill there is another track junction. The GOW turns right (turning left takes you for a short detour into the picturesque Ryans Den GOW campground for wonderful views back east to Bowker Point from the far end of the campground – and another terrific loo-with-a-view). FOR CAMPERS, go straight ahead at the GOW track junction to start your day.

Bit of a steep climb

7.2 The GOW winds through the bush then starts a long slog up to Cape Volney past a line of whispering she-oaks in a wide cleared paddock. Stop to catch your breath (more than once, even!) and look back to see how far you have come. (Just after the fenceless stile and before the fire access gate,

View to Point Reginald

at the GOW track marker, there is an overgrown track to the right, *Cape Volney Track*, which is a 1.8-kilometre exit route to Great Ocean Road from this remote stretch in an emergency.) Otherwise, continue straight ahead along the GOW, past the old seat, for open views in every direction.

No rest on Cape Volney

7.3 The track descends steadily (very slippery when wet) then turns inland to cross a footbridge over a little stream. As the track starts up again, look for a break in the shrubs on the left and clamber up for a great view of a random knobbly land-bound sandstone stack (a lost Apostle perhaps?). Continue uphill once more to be rewarded with two solid seats to rest your weary feet/lungs at the Moonlight Head lookout and views back to Point Reginald.

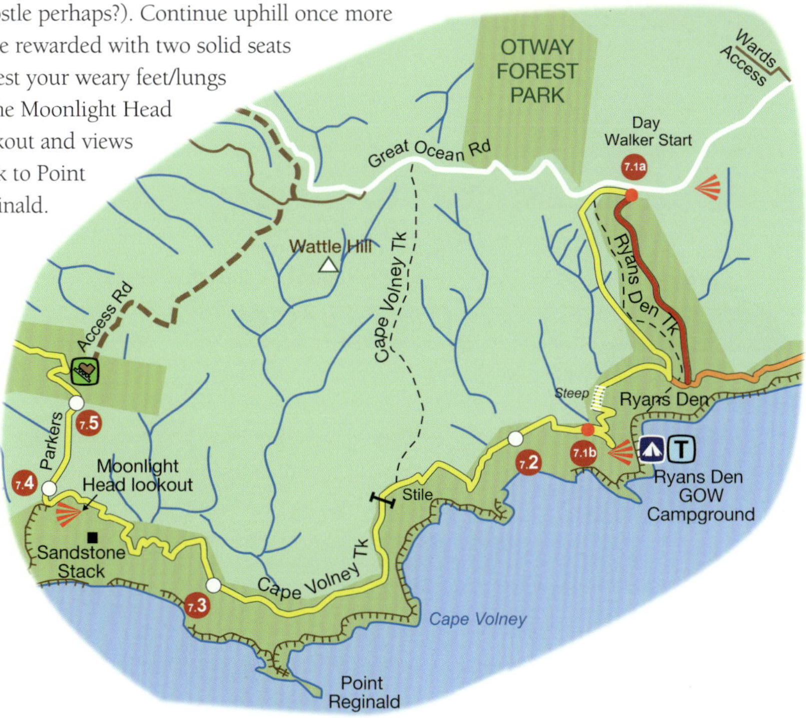

Day 7

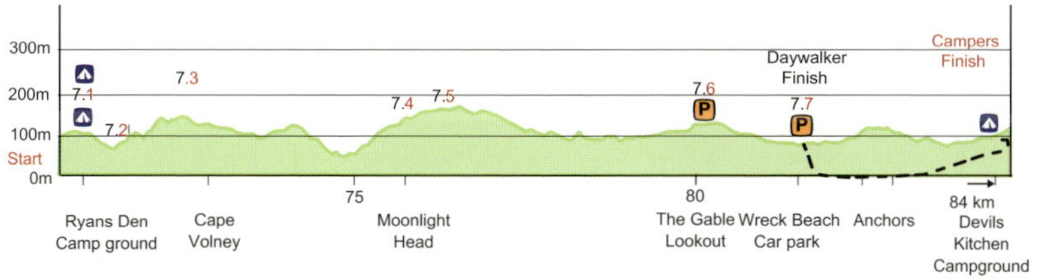

Day 7 Ryans Den to Devils Kitchen/Wreck Beach

7.4 From the lookout, the track continues a short way before turning right. Head over a locked low bar/gate to emerge beside farmland and then go through a gate to join the *Parker Access Track*. Follow the walker's path straight ahead which runs parallel to the dirt road on the right and the farm fence on the left, signed *Gables car park 4.5 km*.

7.5 After 500 metres, the track turns sharp left, away from the road, over a stile and via a boot cleaning station into sheltered bushland and a pleasingly flat stretch. The GOW meanders gently though mixed shrubs and eucalypts, fern gullies, along board walks and, in winter, amazing fungi. There is another boot cleaning station as you emerge from this section.

7.6 At the T-junction you have the option of turning right to walk for 200 meters through the Gables car park (also an optional exit point for the day) and up the dirt road for a further 500 meters to visit the remote Moonlight Head Cemetery (est. 1905). Otherwise, you can turn left for the short detour out to The Gables Lookout or continue straight ahead along the GOW for an easy 1.2-kilometre walk through low coastal scrub to the Wreck Beach car park, which is the suggested exit point **FOR DAY WALKERS**.

7.7 **FOR CAMPERS**, continue through the Wreck Beach car park and along the GOW for a further 2.9 kilometres, with three boot cleaning stations en route, before reaching Devils Kitchen GOW Campground which is perched high above the Devils Kitchen natural landslip/amphitheatre, well back from the coastline.

Gentle boardwalks through the forest

Moonlight Head Cemetery gatehouse

Wreck Beach 'anchor' detour

One of the highlights of the Great Ocean Walk is to see the famous anchors of the *Marie Gabrielle* and *Fiji* shipwrecks in their rugged and remote settings. If you arrive at Wreck Beach with time to spare and outgoing/low tides, you can take the 366 steps (slippery when wet) down onto the soft sand of Wreck Beach. The beach is completely covered at high tide and is bordered by 20-50 m high cliffs so don't take risks on incoming tides or stormy seas. On the sand, turn right to discover the anchor and other remnants of the wreck of the *Marie Gabrielle* (1869) lodged into the rockpools on the edge of the beach at the end of the first bay. A further 100 metres along, around the little point, you will discover the anchor of the *Fiji* (1891), secured at the bottom of the cliffs in a base of concrete. Take time to look up the daunting cliff face at this point, as this is where the survivors of the *Fiji* (and the bodies of those who tragically lost their lives in the dramatic rescue) were hauled up the cliff on pulleys. Day walkers can backtrack to the car park for pick-up. For campers, you can choose to continue along the beach and ascend up the steep, uneven track to the Devils Kitchen GOW campground via the Devils Kitchen, but it is a much harder walk in soft sand with packs than the inland route. A better option is to take the inland track to the Campground, then descend to Wreck Beach without your packs after you have set up, or before leaving in the morning (tide dependant), or to do a quick side trip up and down the stairs from Wreck Beach car park before continuing along the inland track.

Fiji's 'lost' Memorial and gravesite at Moonlight Head

Victorian historian, Alan McLean, has led a tireless campaign for the preservation and restoration of the 'lost' Fiji Shipwreck disaster memorial stone which was built on the edge of the cliff above the site of the actual shipwreck along Wreck Beach and near the resting place of some of those who drowned. For decades, the memorial was surrounded by dense bush and forgotten. As a result of the efforts of Alan and his good friend, Brian Salmon, whose father remembered its location and encouraged them to rediscover it, it is now easily accessible as a short, marked side trip off the track.

Alan's story of the wrecking of the *Fiji* in 1891, the tragic loss of 11 of its crew and a brave local rescuer, the dramatic rescue of survivors, including a naked German found wandering in the bush, and the looting (and subsequent imbibing!) of its cargo by locals, makes for a riveting and meticulously researched read (*Mystery at Moonlight Head: The Fiji Shipwreck Disaster of 1891*).

Fiji Shipwreck Memorial

Alternate routes

Parks Victoria recommends the use of only the ***GOW inland*** route options where these options are available. Alternate routes along the beaches and rock platforms are officially signed, but can potentially be quite dangerous. Decision Point numbering/naming aligns with the official map/signage.

GOW Official Decision Point	Description/location	Conditions	Exit/escape options
Wreck Beach Decision Point **11A**	1.5 km beachwalk. Access at low and outgoing tides only via a long staircase (366 steps) from the Wreck Beach car park and the path up to Devils Kitchen, 1.5 km away.	The soft sandy beaches here disappear entirely at high tide and are edged by high sea cliffs. Even at low tide, watch for freak waves and deep rockpools when on the anchor rock platforms.	Only escape routes are via the Wreck Beach car park staircase and the path up to Devils Kitchen.

Day 8 Devils Kitchen/Wreck Beach to the Twelve Apostles

At a glance

Distance: 15.2 km (camping), 18.1 km (day walk)

Time: 5-6 hours

Difficulty: Easy

Highlights: Wreck Beach anchors, Gellibrand River, dune-top approach to the Twelve Apostles

The final day of the Walk is upon you, and it offers a different aspect again – this time running largely along the exposed ridges of sand dunes as you near your destination. This provides a progressively emerging and rewarding view of the Twelve Apostles which are visible for almost half of your walk. Getting closer, the eventual re-entry into the hubbub of the Twelve Apostles visitor areas may be a little overwhelming for some after the peace of the GOW to this point. There are lots of options on this section: some more leisurely walkers choose to stop overnight at Gellibrand River/Princetown to extend their walk another night so they can finish early on the last day to make bus timetables and the trip back to Melbourne or beyond easily in the same day; some push through to the end and take a helicopter ride to see where they have come from; some take transport into pretty Port Campbell for a last celebratory night together there, visiting Loch Ard Gorge on the way. While Port Campbell is just 11 kilometres from the Twelve Apostles, there is currently no safe walking route to get there – sadly, the only choice (unsafe and not recommended) is the narrow hard shoulder of the very busy Great Ocean Road. There are long-held plans to eventually extend the walk into Port Campbell, which would make so much sense, but this is unfortunately many years away. Whichever way you choose to do it, it will be a fitting end to your extraordinary walk.

Gellibrand Estuary

Day 8 Devils Kitchen/Wreck Beach to the Twelve Apostles

	Start	Finish	
Camping option	Devils Kitchen GOW Campground	Twelve Apostles	15.2 km
Day walk option	Wreck Beach car park	Twelve Apostles	18.1 km

More boot cleaning

Walk directions

8.1a FOR DAY WALKERS, from the Wreck Beach car park, head north along the GOW passing through the first of the day's boot cleaning stations and a relatively straight forward 2.9-kilometre walk through mixed coastal heathlands, along boardwalks, up staircases and above the natural amphitheatre of Devils Kitchen to pass Devils Kitchen GOW Campground. Alternatively, if the tide is very low/outgoing (and you didn't get the chance to visit the shipwreck anchors along Wreck Beach the previous day – refer Day 7 box), you can head down the 366 steps to Wreck Beach and turn right to take the alternate beach route. This will involve the same distance as the inland route, but on soft sand and with either a steep scramble at the end of the beach to regain the GOW or turn back up the Wreck Beach steps. Allow a good hour to explore the wrecks.

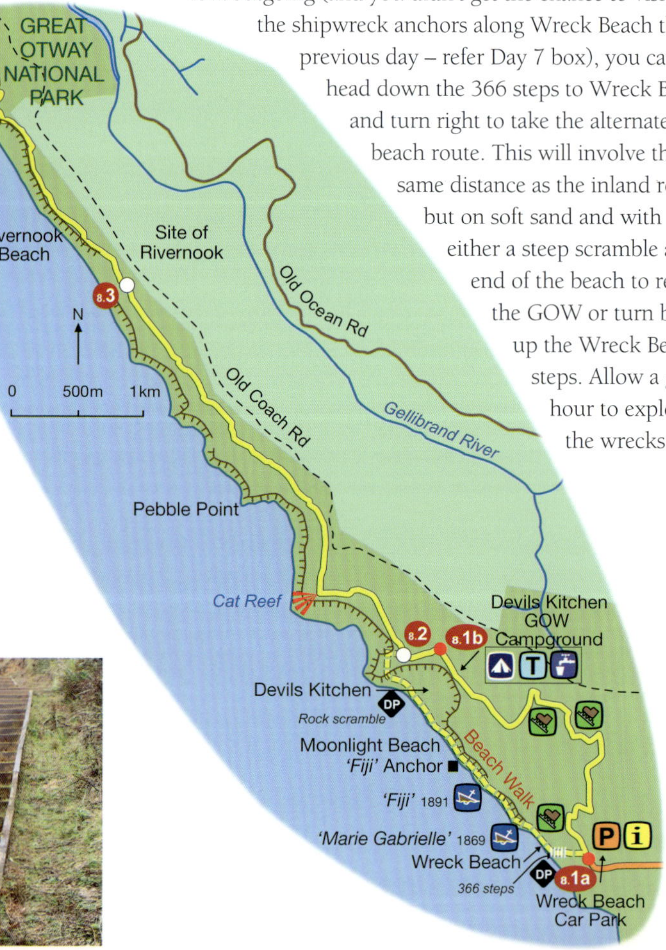

8.1b FOR CAMPERS, if you came the main inland route to the Devils Kitchen GOW Campground, and it is low/outgoing tide, you could carry along the GOW and take the steep and uneven detour down to the beach without your packs, turning left along the soft sand, to have a look at the anchors of the *Fiji* and *Marie Gabrielle* before returning to the campground to pack up and set out for the day.

8.2 Back on the GOW, past the Devils Kitchen Campground, continue straight ahead at the sign *12 Apostles 15.4 km*. Turn left at the next boot cleaning station (ignoring the track straight ahead to *Old Coach Road*), continuing straight ahead, past the track up from Wreck Beach on the left. When the view opens out, there is a well-placed seat which provides your first view of the Twelve Apostles in the distance.

Down over the dunes to Gellibrand River

Rivernook Beach and Point Ronald beyond

8.3 Keep a lookout for the large remnant Cyprus trees on the right as you walk above Rivernook Beach, indicating the site of the famous Rivernook Guesthouse (see box). Continue ahead, crossing over a vehicle turnaround and road (signed *Gellibrand River car park 3.1 km*). The vegetation changes noticeably from this point and the path underfoot becomes rocky limestone and then quite sandy before you start to descend on the duckboard down to Gellibrand River.

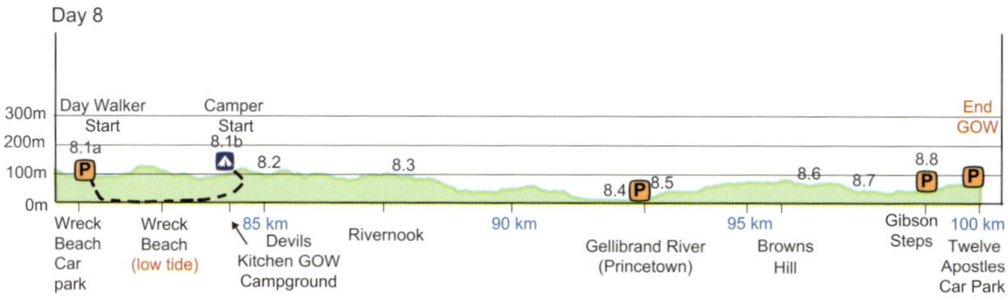

8.4 When you reach the river, turn right (or left if you want to do a return detour to Princetown Beach and get a close up look at Point Ronald headland at the river mouth). Walk through the car park along the dirt vehicle track beside the river, passing Princetown Recreation Reserve on your right. Cross over the Gellibrand River bridge, leaving Cape Otway National Park behind. To your right there is an extensive boardwalk across Latrobe Creek and through the wetlands reserve which takes you on a pleasant detour to the little hilltop village of Princetown. Sometimes there is a general store/post office and/or tavern open here, along with lovely views over the wetlands and Gellibrand River, but it is best to call ahead to confirm they are open as business openings are seasonal. Some walkers may choose to break their walk here overnight, as there are a number of accommodation options (which should be booked in advance).

8.5 Back at the bridge, the GOW track continues to the left, past the information board and up and over the hill, as you now enter Port Campbell National Park. The last few kilometres take you along the ridges of the sand dunes along a sheltered track as you gain height for lovely views back across Princetown and forward to your destination.

Competition on the Princetown boardwalk

Over the dunes

8.6 At the old stile (now fenceless) across the sandy 4WD track, there is a nice detour down to Clifton Beach: the hidden path goes down at the *Beach* sign on the right side of the clearing as you look at the sea.

8.7 Back on the GOW, continue along the undulating boardwalk/track. Don't miss the iconic GOW photo opportunity at the scenic lookout. It's a few steps off the track to the left and easy to miss for those focussed on the main goal! Take a moment to breathe before you reenter civilisation: the buzz of helicopters and tour buses can be quite overwhelming after only the sound of waves for the last week. From here, head down the stone steps and turn sharp left (signed *GOW039*) not straight ahead (this was the original no-fuss finish of the GOW which just turfed you out unceremoniously on the road, opposite historic Glenample Homestead).

Day 8 Devils Kitchen/Wreck Beach to the Twelve Apostles

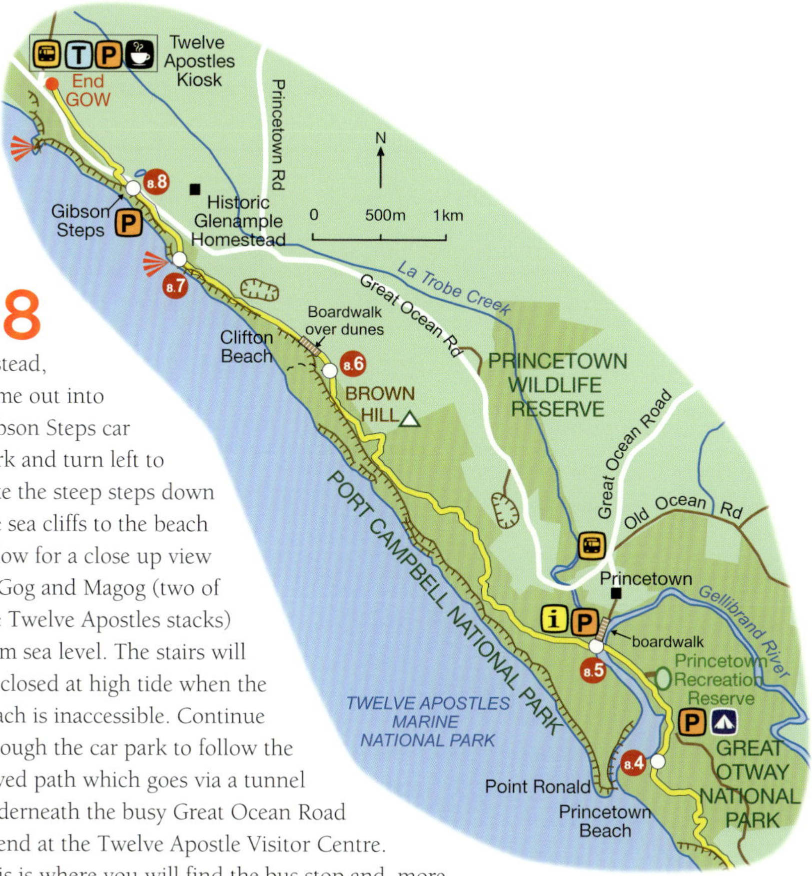

8.8

Instead, come out into Gibson Steps car park and turn left to take the steep steps down the sea cliffs to the beach below for a close up view of Gog and Magog (two of the Twelve Apostles stacks) from sea level. The stairs will be closed at high tide when the beach is inaccessible. Continue through the car park to follow the paved path which goes via a tunnel underneath the busy Great Ocean Road to end at the Twelve Apostle Visitor Centre. This is where you will find the bus stop and, more importantly, the ice-cream fridge and barista coffee! Before you go, don't miss the short walk out to the scenic viewing platforms for the entire Twelve Apostles scenic experience. Congratulations, you made it!

Made it

Day 8 Devils Kitchen/Wreck Beach to the Twelve Apostles

Alternate routes

Parks Victoria recommends the use of only the ***GOW inland*** route options where these options are available. Alternate routes along the beaches and rock platforms are officially signed, but can potentially be quite dangerous. Where it is quite unwise, regardless of tides, even for experienced and highly capable walkers, we have indicated 'not recommended'. Decision Point numbering/ naming aligns with the official map/signage.

GOW Official Decision Point	Description/location	Conditions	Exit/escape options
Wreck Beach Decision Point **11A**	Wreck and Moonlight Beaches. Access via Wreck Beach car park staircase.	Soft sand walking, rock platforms, some rock scrambling at end of Wreck Beach to climb out. Beach is entirely covered at high tide.	None for 1.5km (at end of beach), so make sure you have plenty of time.
Wreck Beach Decision Point **11B**	Devils Kitchen access to Moonlight Beach.	Bordered by high sea cliffs and covered by water on rising tides, scrambling, rock platforms and gullies.	Not recommended. No exit before Rivernook beach.

Gellibrand and the Gadubanud

The Gellibrand River is named after the first Attorney General of Van Diemen's Land (later, Tasmania), Joseph Gellibrand, who unsuccessfully petitioned the Governor, Arthur Phillip, to introduce a trial system in the colony's courts and lost his job as a result. Gellibrand later was involved in the Port Philip Association which sought to negotiate the Batman Treaty with the Wirandjuri people, for assignment of their land around present-day Melbourne, in return for annual provisions for the Traditional Owners, but it was overturned by the Governor. Undeterred, Gellibrand spent time exploring the western districts with his Hobart friend, George Hesse. In 1837, they disappeared without trace while somewhere in the forests near Birregurra. Despite a number of rescue attempts they were never found alive. However, subsequent research into their disappearance indicated that they did in fact become lost in the dense Otways forests. Reportedly, Hesse died of exposure or starvation, but Gellibrand was rescued by the coastal Gadubanud people who cared for him for some months until he was strangled in a fight with a rival clan. The Gadubanud buried him near the mouth of the Gellibrand River. Latrobe referred to the grave in his own explorations and Gellibrand's remains were later exhumed in 1844 by a local Warrnambool pastoralist, with the help of Gadubanud guides, and returned to his family in Hobart.

Rivernook Guest House

Rivernook

As you walk along the clifftops between Devils Kitchen and the Gellibrand River, above Rivernook Beach, on the right hand side you will pass some very out-of-place large Cyprus trees. This is all the remaining evidence of what was once the vibrant and popular Victorianera Rivernook Guesthouse run by Mr and Mrs Evans. The Guesthouse was really a resort of its day, and a very popular destination for the gentry of Ballarat and surrounds. The Guesthouse played an important role in the rescue of the *Fiji* survivors, with guests generously providing clothing and the proprietors hosting and feeding many of the traumatised and exhausted sailors for some time until they were recovered enough to travel to Port Campbell.

Rivernook guests

Geology: The Seven, Eight, Twelve Apostles

Base of the Gibson Steps

Dawn at the Twelve Apostles

Geology: The Seven, Eight, Twelve Apostles

The so-called Twelve Apostles are made up of a soft limestone, known as Port Campbell limestone, which was deposited between 15 and 5 million years ago, in the mid-late Miocene period. Many visitors are confused not to actually see 12 stacks from the viewpoints, and in fact there were only ever eight stacks in this immediate vicinity, with others further to the west. The rugged weather and pounding Southern Ocean are responsible for the ongoing erosion of the stacks, which commence as caves gouged into the sea cliffs punch through promontories to become arches, which in turn collapse. Walkers old enough may remember the 'London Bridge' collapse of 1990 which left two people stranded on what is now known as 'London Arch', a little further along the coastline near Loch Ard. In 2005, one of the eight original stacks also collapsed into the sea, leaving only seven Apostles now standing. Nevertheless, at up to 50 metres high, they are an impressive sight in any weather and at low tide you can even walk down the Gibson Steps to the beach (because you haven't had enough GOW steps yet!) for an entirely different perspective.

Walking beyond the Great Ocean Walk

Thunder Cave

While there is a vision for the GOW to be extended from the Twelve Apostles west to Port Campbell, it is unlikely to happen any time soon. However, for those with their own transport, it is really worth spending a day or more exploring the spectacular Port Campbell National Park coastline further west of the Twelve Apostles. The Loch Ard Gorge area has a wide variety of short scenic walks, including the aptly-named Thunder Cave where the powerful ocean swell pushes violently up through a tunnel and crashes loudly onto rocks before surging out again. The *Wreck of the Loch Ard Walk* down into Loch Ard Gorge itself and, if at low tide, onto the beach and cave, reveals the tragic and redemptive tale of the wrecking of the *Loch Ard* which ran aground in heavy mist near Mutton Bird Island, just offshore, in 1878. There were only two survivors, both of whom were just 19 years old: ship's apprentice Tom Pearce and Irish immigrant Eva Carmichael who he rescued from the waters. The sandstone stacks at the entrance to Loch Ard, now officially called Tom and Eva, were once an archway. There is also a longer walk which takes you out and

Loch Ard Gorge

along the wild coastline. All the walks are well signed with interpretive information boards. Mutton birds return to their nests at dusk on Mutton Bird Island in their thousands, and the best times to see them are in January-February — there is a lookout platform here for viewing.

Port Campbell, 10 kilometres beyond the Apostles, is a pretty fishing and popular holiday village, built around a protected cove and is home to the *Port Campbell Discovery Walk to Two Mile Bay* (4 and 6 km options). There is also a fascinating display of shipwreck artefacts and information in the Port Campbell Visitor Information Centre.

Beyond Port Campbell, you will find London Arch, which until 1990 was known as London Bridge. Older Australian hikers might recall the news bulletins showing the collapse of the original arch, leaving two tourists stranded out on the sandstone stack which was left. It was some hours before a police helicopter was able to rescue them. It is no surprise how unstable and ever-changing this landscape is when you see the way the ocean pounds the coastline, with the spray from the waves sometimes reaching over the top of the cliffs.

The next little township is Peterborough, which has a 4-kilometre clifftop heathland walking track around its promontory and is the starting point for the Bay of Islands Coastal Park, which includes the Bay of Martyrs and stretches as far as the Logan Beach Southern Right whale nursery in Warnambool (winter whale watching heaven). For those not yet done stretching their legs, there is a 37 kilometre rail trail which travels from Warnambool's Lake Pertobe, via Koroit and Levys Point to the Moyne River in picturesque Port Fairy.

West beyond Loch Ard

Safety Tips

It is important not to overstate the danger of Australia's outdoors, which is generally very safe. Being aware of potential hazards though, makes good sense. While some of the GOW is in relatively accessible areas, some days are very remote and isolated, so for your personal safety, and that of your friends or any emergency personnel who might have to be involved in any rescue, please keep in mind the following common-sense guidelines.

General

It's always advisable (and more fun!) to walk with companions, although the GOW is also very doable solo. Carry a mobile phone with good coverage — note that not all providers will have coverage of all the walks areas — Telstra is generally better, but even so **there are some sections of the walk which do not have any mobile phone coverage**. For that reason, and given many sections of the GOW are remote and inaccessible, every group should carry at least one Personal Locator Beacon, preferably with messaging capabilities. Garmin Inreach is a lightweight example which also allows you to send short messages. They can be hired from some outdoor stores. Pack a small first aid kit (including 1-2 pressure bandages for snakebite). Tell someone reliable of your walk plans, and what time you expect to finish, so that if needed people will know where to start looking for you — this is particularly important if you are walking solo. Use the Victoria Police Trip Intentions Form (www.police.vic.gov.au/outdoor-and-bush-safety#trip-intentions-form). Take particular care near water, roads, beaches, rock platforms, river crossings and the many crumbling cliff edges. If walking

with children (the GOW is a great multiday walk for teenagers due to its variety and shorter distances), keep a close eye on them at all times.

Weather

After a storm!

The weather in southern Victoria can be notoriously unpredictable, and it is not uncommon for the temperature gauge to drop 10 degrees in a matter of minutes. Be prepared for all weathers when you set out, as even a sunny warm day can turn into howling gales and rain, and many of the days in the second half of the Walk in particular are quite exposed. Always carry warm clothing and rainproof gear, even if you set out on a hot and sunny day. In the forested areas of the Walk, falling tree branches can be a real danger in high winds.

Sun, water and heat-related illnesses

Victoria's summers can be very hot, dry and the sun unforgiving. Sunburn can be painful and is the main cause of skin cancer in later life. It is easy to become dehydrated so take plenty of water, at least one litre per person for every two hours walking in summer, and remember there is no potable or even many reliable sources of water along the Walk each day to stock up on should you run out. Water at campsites is untreated and intended for campers only. Quite a few of the days, particularly in the second half of the GOW, are very exposed with little shade, so ensure you rest when you do find some shade and even on cool days, wear a hat with a brim, clothes which will protect you from sunburn and use lots of sunscreen. On days of extreme heat, if you must walk, set off very early in the morning or late afternoon and make the most of the extended summer daylight hours. Be aware of heat-related illness which can come on very quickly.

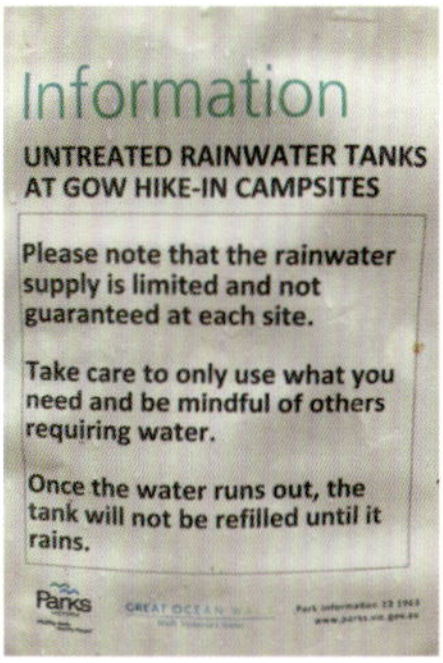

Safety Tips

For a very good tabulated summary regarding the effects of heat, on what to be on the lookout for and how to best react to any symptoms, Queensland Health has a very good webpage: https://www.health.qld.gov.au/news-events/news/difference-between-heat-exhaustion-and-heat-stroke-dehydration-heatwave .

River crossing

Tides

Many of the walks in this book include sections of beach walking and some river mouth crossings which can only be done at low or outgoing tides. The walk notes in this book indicate if beach sections can only be undertaken at low tide. Take care to check the tide times very carefully, including calculating adjustments for the area, in advance of your walk. Aim to ensure you are doing any river crossings or beachwalk sections on outgoing and low tides only. If in doubt, DO NOT undertake beach or rock platform sections if waves are rough or tides are high or incoming and there is a risk you may be trapped, or washed off rocks — an inland alternative is indicated if conditions are unsafe. There are some sections of beach and some river crossings, which are clearly indicated, where no inland alternative is available. If in doubt, DO NOT under any circumstances cross, but either wait for the tide to turn and water to receded, or return and retrace your steps, taking inland options where available, or if not, come back another day in more favourable conditions. All the beaches of the walk face the wild Southern Ocean, with unpredictable waves, huge swells and are lined with crumbling vertical cliffs, limiting escape options should you become trapped, so please do not take this warning lightly.

When checking tide times, ensure you look at the times for your closest reference point (eg Apollo Bay, Cape Otway, Princetown). Times can vary substantially along this coast, with large tidal variations affected by the Southern Ocean swells, moon cycle, seasons and storm activity. Good regional daily information is available from the Bureau of Meteorology or from Willy Weather.

Swimming

While the blue ocean and pristine beaches can be very tempting on hot days, almost all of the beaches along the GOW are dangerous, with permanent rips and powerful waves, even on calm days. Even Johanna Beach, a surfing mecca, has eight permanent rips – and you need to learn how to identify and avoid them. It's a good idea to check each beach on www.beachsafe.org.au for details of known rips, undertows and currents. Outside of lifesaver patrolled beaches (ie. most beaches on this walk), there is no one to rescue you if you get into trouble. In fresh water and at river mouth crossings, beware of underwater hazards and cold water currents, particularly after rain or recent flood. Under no circumstances should you swim or venture into flood-swollen rivers, so your option may be to take an alternate inland route, where available, or to sit and wait till waters recede. Be conscious that at some of the river crossings along the GOW you will potentially be contending with an outflow of water from the river as well as wave action inflow from the ocean, plus shifting sands, which can make crossings unpredictable.

Bushfires

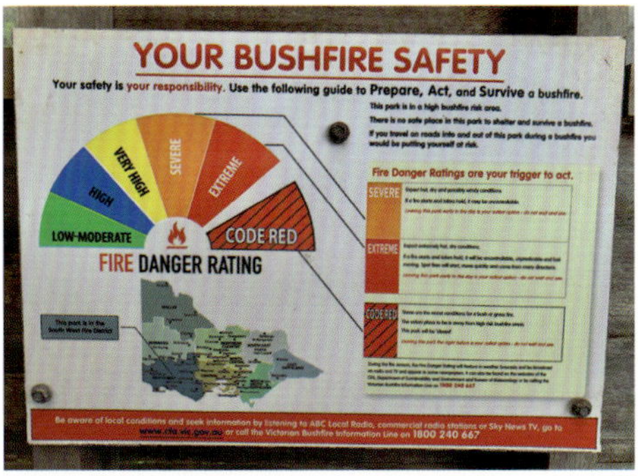

The Christmas Day bushfires of 2015, which affected the Otways region, were a harsh reminder of the risks born by those living in and near such magnificent bushlands. Bushfires are a genuine hazard in Victoria during summer and the advice and warnings given must be heeded. Be extremely conscious of not flicking matches, embers or cigarettes on the ground. Cooking at GOW campsites can only be done with fuel stoves. No open fires are allowed at any time of year. On days of Code Red fire danger rating, all of the State's parks will be closed for public safety as fires can move incredibly fast and be unpredictable.

Due to the remote nature of the walk, you may not be notified if a Code Red day is called, but you have a responsibility to stay informed and move out of the area in advance. Don't second guess yourself; as Victorians know from tragic experience, you cannot outrun a bushfire.

Safety Tips

We have listed all possible exit routes from the Walk in the Build Your Own Walk table. Out of fire season, the government may conduct controlled burns in some areas with an aim to reduce fuel load. **Check Emergency Victoria's website before setting out on your walk to check for current fire warnings and planned burns: http://emergency.vic.gov.au/respond.** Some hikers also carry small portable radios so they can listen to any emergency broadcasting when out of phone range. ABC 774AM is the local emergency station.

Snakes

Despite all the hype, it is important to understand that snakes are far more frightened of you (enormous, loud human!) than you are of them, and will do everything they can to avoid and escape from you. It is quite common on the Great Ocean Walk, at any time of the year when the sun is out, but particularly in the summer, to come across a snake basking in the sun in the middle of the track. Along the GOW they are likely to be either tiger (which may or may not have banded markings) or eastern brown snakes, both highly venomous and whose bites can be fatal. If you are lucky, you may also see the more shy red bellied black snakes. If you do see a snake: stop still, wait for it to move, or walk quietly and slowly away from it and allow it to slide away. Under NO circumstances should you try and approach it, frighten it or kill it. Apart from the fact that they are protected, 95% of all snake bites in Australia occur as a result of people trying to kill snakes. It is a good idea to wear long trousers, sturdy shoes and even gaiters, while walking in Australia, and to keep your eyes on the ground while walking, so you don't inadvertently step on one.

In the VERY unlikely case that you should get bitten, the most important thing is to NOT PANIC. Panic can speed the spread of any venom. Many snakebites do not result in venom being released, but you should treat ALL bites as though they *have* been envenomated. DO NOT suck, cut or wipe the wound as a swab will be taken to identify the right antivenom. DO NOT use a tourniquet —

Tiger snake

you are more likely to lose your limb to gangrene than to the bite! DO NOT try and catch or kill the snake for identification. **Here's what the St John's Ambulance recommends you DO in the event of a snake bite**:

1. Reassure the person who has been bitten, keeping them as calm as possible.
2. Apply a pressure immobilisation bandage:
   - Wrap a broad bandage around the bite area as soon as possible.
   - Apply a firm, heavy elasticised (compression) bandage just above the fingers or toes and work your way upwards on the limb, over the top of clothes is fine. Wrap the bandage past the snake bite and as far up the limb as possible.
   - Ensure the bandage is applied firmly without hindering blood circulation.
3. Splint the bandaged limb to help keep it still, if it is a leg — you can bandage it to the other leg.
4. Ensure the patient remains still. Try and protect them from the weather where possible without moving them.
5. Call triple zero (000) for medical assistance or activate your PLB if you are out of mobile range. Be prepared to give accurate information about your whereabouts so that you can be located as quickly as possible. The GOW is marked regularly with Emergency Markers (GW001, GW002 etc) which will provide a reference number for emergency services to help find you.
6. Record the time the bite occurred and when the bandage was applied (if possible, mark the site of the bite on the bandage with a pen).
7. Wait with the casualty, monitor and record any changes in their condition. Do not move them unless instructed by emergency services personnel to do so.
8. In a worse-case scenario, if the patient collapses due to the venom travelling through their lymph system and does not seem to be breathing, you must be prepared to administer CPR (30 compressions: 2 breaths) until they start breathing or help arrives.

(Source: https://www.stjohnvic.com.au/news/snake-bite-first-aid-tips)

For those interested in learning more about Australia's incredible snakes, there are some excellent Facebook pages run by respected herpetologists, conservationists and wildlife rescuers, which are educative, respectful and very helpful, including: *Fast Snake Identification (Australia Wide)* if you have a photo of a snake you have encountered and want a positive ID, and *Wildlife Awareness Australia* if you have general questions about snakes, reptiles and other Australian wildlife.

Safety Tips

Leeches

Leeches are a common annoyance in wetter areas along the GOW, but will usually brush off or drop off once full, or you can slide a credit card or knife blade under their sucker to encourage them to drop off. While painless, leeches inject an anti-coagulant into the skin, which can cause bleeding and itchiness when they drop off. Just apply pressure with a finger or band-aid and it will soon stop. Do not pull them off, as, like ticks, this can cause them to leave their teeth behind in the skin, causing infection. Clean the site with an antiseptic and cover it with a sticking plaster to avoid this. Some people can react to multiple leech bites, so it's not a bad idea to carry an anti-histamine. Wearing long trousers or gaiters can reduce the potential for leeches and ticks to attach, as can spraying your socks and trousers with Aeroguard, Bushman's or similar, and tucking your socks into your trousers (not a great look, but effective!). Do check all over your body at the end of each day, as they can get in the most unsavoury and unexpected places — dark and moist is their favourite!

Other annoyances

Southern Blue-Ringed Octopus

At beaches and rockpools do not to pick up pretty little blue ringed octopuses, which may be shy and rare but are extremely venomous (fatal). It is also advisable to check both your skin and scalp for bush ticks after each day, which should not be left untreated in the skin, but removed gently, taking care not to leave the head attached. Tea-tree oil can be a deterrent. Horse flies can be a nuisance in summer on hot days. They are attracted to blue clothing, and deterred somewhat by insect repellent. Swinging your poles wildly around your head and swearing violently does not seem to work, I have found, though it may make you feel better and provide endless entertainment for your fellow hikers.

Pelican

Regional Wildlife

The wilder weather of the Southern Ocean coastline, along with clay and sandy soils, make for challenging conditions for local wildlife. And these have only been made harder by highly effective feral predators such as introduced foxes, dogs and cats. Many of the marsupials are nocturnal and will often be heard in the evenings by those camping, rather than being spotted during the day. There is nothing quite like the loud grunting and roaring of mating koalas at night to grab your attention when you are just about to nod off! If you are lucky enough to spot rare and endangered animals such as the Spotted Quoll or Long Nosed Potoroo, which are being carefully reintroduced in Cape Otway, please do report your sightings (ideally with photographic evidence) to the Cape Otway Conservation Ecology Centre (www.conservationecologycentre.org). There are of course some species which are thriving, including Tiger and Eastern brown snakes, kangaroos (which can be spotted in open areas), koalas (often at Blanket Bay and Aire River) and Australian fur seals (commonly spotted in Apollo Bay, Cape Marengo and beyond). The smallest of creatures flourish in the rockpools and moist fern tree gullies along the route; the tiny 2 cm long Otway Black Snail is found nowhere else on earth. The more quietly you traverse the land, the higher the likelihood of spotting and enjoying some of this region's diverse fauna, some of which is pictured here.

Australian fur seal
Arctocephalus pusillus

Butterfly: Australian/ Yellow Admiral
Vanessa itea

Butterfly: Swordgrass brown
Tisiphone Abeona

Canary Worm
Fletchamia sugdeni

Eastern Blue tongue lizard, *Tiliqua scincoides scincoides*

Tiger snake
Notechis scutatus

For those interested in learning more: Cape Otway Conservation Ecology Centre www.conservation ecologycentre.org

Echidna (short-beaked)
Tachyglossus aculeatus

Eight armed sea star
Meridiastra calcar

Garden skink ('Droptail')
Lampropholis guichenoti

Koala, *Phascolarctos cinereus*

Waratah Anenomes
Actinia tenebrosa

Long nosed potoroo
Potorus tridactylus

Otway black snail
Victaphanta compacta

Platypus
Ornithorhynchus anatinus

Spotted or Tiger quoll
Dasyurus maculatus

Swamp wallaby
Wallabia bicolour

Eastern grey kangaroo
Macropus giganteus

Bush Rat
Rattus-fuscipes

Regional Birdlife

You are likely to see a wide range of beautiful and some quite rare Australian native birds, which frequent the many varied habitats — from rainforest fern gullies, to tall eucalypt woodlands, to coastal shrubs and heathland — along the Great Ocean Walk. Take the time to just sit quietly and see what you might hear and see. Just a few of the birds you might encounter are shown below. For more information, we recommend www.birdingvictoria.com.au (the Western Victoria — Otways and Great Ocean Road section) and *The Slater Field Guide to Australian Birds*.

Pink Robin, *Petroica rodinogaster (11-13 cm)*

Scarlet Robin, *Petroica multicolour (12-14 cm)*

Spotted Pardalot, *Pardalotus punctatus (8-10 cm)*

Grey Fantail, *Rhipidura fuliginosa (14-17 cm)*

Willy Wagtail, *Rhipidura leucophrys (19-22 cm)*

Silvereye, *Zosterops lateralis (10-12 cm)*

Superb Fairy-wren, *Malurus cyaneus (13-14 cm)*

Singing Honeyeater, *Lichenostomus virescens (18-22 cm)*

New Holland Honeyeater, *Phylidonyris novaehollandiae (17-18 cm)*

Musk Lorikeet, *Glossopsitta concinna (20-23 cm)*

Rainbow Lorikeet, *Trichoglossus haematodus (25-32 cm)*

Crimson Rosella (juvenile), *Platycercus elegans (32-37 cm)*

Crimson Rosella (adult), *Platycercus elegans* (32-37 cm)

King Parrot, *Alisterus scapularis* (41-44 cm)

Laughing kookaburra, *Dacelo novaeguineae* (41-47 cm)

Sacred Kingfisher *Todiramphus sanctus* (20-23 cm)

Gang Gang Cockatoo *Callocephalon fimbriantum* (33-36 cm)

Galah, *Cactua roseicapilla* (34-38 cm)

Sulphur Crested Cockatoo *Cacatua galerita* (44-51 cm)

Yellow Tailed Black Cockatoo, *Calyptorhynchus funereus* (55-65 cm)

Tawny Frogmouth *Podargus strigoides* (50-60 cm)

Wedge Tailed Eagle, *Aquila audax (90 cm-1.1 m; wingspan to 2.8 m)*

Buff Banded Rail, *Gallirallus philippensis* (28-33 cm)

Little Pied Cormorant, *Phalacrocorax melanoleucos* (58-64 cm)

Purple swamphen *Porphyrio porphyrio* (44-48 cm)

Royal Spoonbill *Platalea regia* (74-80 cm)

White Faced Heron, *Egretta novaehollandiae* (66-70 cm)

Regional Birdlife

Hooded Plovers: 'Hoodies'

Along the GOW (notably near Johanna Beach, but sometimes elsewhere), if you are very lucky you may see pretty little Hooded Plovers *(Thinornis rubricollis)* scuttering along the shoreline. 'Hoodies' are some of the most endangered and vulnerable birds in Australia and globally. It's not hard to understand why: they lay their camouflaged eggs directly in rocky coastal areas, and on top of the sand on the beach - without a nest to protect them. They are of course above the high tide line, where dogs, birds, other predators and clumsy human feet mean they have a less than 1 in 100 chance of survival. If disturbed by humans, parents will often desert their 'nests' or fragile chicks as they are too frightened to return, or to take their fledglings to the water's edge to feed. Despite this, you have to admire their pluck: even if their nests do fail, breeding pairs will try up to four times in a season (September to March) to succeed. However, all is not lost - with help from organisations like Birdlife Australia, Parks Victoria and the Great Ocean Road Coast and Parks Authority, as well as passionate local volunteer groups, numbers have in fact increased in the last few years, from a low of 200 in Victoria a few years ago to around 550 now. If you see any signs, nesting shelters or fences, please stay clear and watch where you are walking on the beach sections! You can find out more from www.birdlife.org.au/projects/beaches-nesting-birds an organisation which welcomes volunteers. They have a really informative 'Hoodies' YouTube clip available: https://youtu.be/-hl8eYh7_rl.

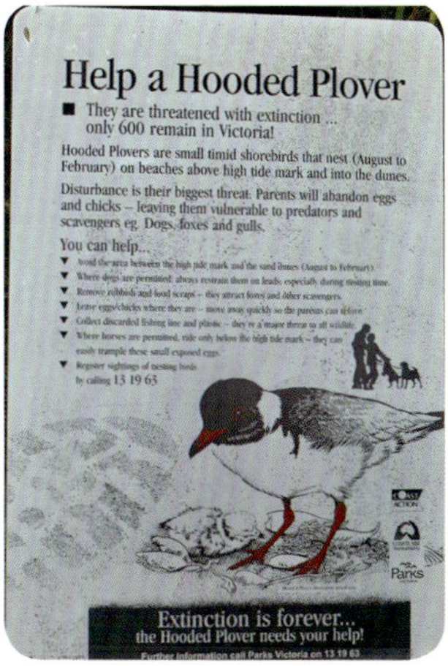

Regional Flora

The biodiversity along this relatively small section of Victoria's southern coastline is a real feature of the Walk, and this is reflected in the variety of plant life along the way. The GOW will take you through tall wet eucalypt forests of mountain ash — the tallest flowering tree in the world, messmate forests with beautiful orchids, cool temperate rainforests with lush fern tree gullies, grass tree forests, dry coastal heathlands, fragile sand dune vegetation, estuaries with rich marshlands and more. At different times of the year the GOW can look entirely different, thanks to the ever-changing backdrop of beautiful native flowers, colourful fungi, and the dramatic seasonality of the weather. We have listed some of the flowers you might find along the way, though there will be many more. We have also shown some of the common classified weed flowers you might come across — they may be beautiful but are noxious pests in the area. Please be conscious of not spreading their foliage, seeds or flowers. *See next page for photo chart.*

Below: Common weeds (non-natives) - take care not to spread them, pretty as they are.

Sea spurge *Euphorbia paralias*

Cape broom *Genista monspessulana*

Sweet pea bush *Polygala myrtiflora*

Self-heal *Prunella vulgaris*

Regional Flora

Drooping sheoak
Allocasuarina verticillata

Sea box
Alyxia buxifolia

Silver banksia,
Banksia marginata

River rose
Bauera rubiodes

Coast or Beach Daisy
Brachyscome parvula

Coast or Beach Daisy
Brachyscome parvula

Christmas Bush
Bursaria spinosa

Cushion bush
Calocephalus brownii

Karkalla or pig face
Carpobrotus rossii

Old man's beard
Clematis aristata

White correa
Correa alba

Australian fuschia
Correa backhouseana

Tree fern
Dickinsonia Antarctica

Hyacinth orchid
Dipodium roseum

Pink Common Heath
Epacris impressa

Mountain Ash
Eucalyptus regnans

Hop goodenia
Goodenia ovata

Prickly tea-tree
Leptospermum continentale

Coast daisy bush
Olearia axilaris

Twiggy daisy
Olearia ramulosa

Coast everlasting
Ozothamnus turbinatus

Native Iris
Patersonia occidentalis

Seaberry saltbush
Rhagodia canolleana

Fireweed groundsel
enecio linearifolius

Scented Groundsel
Senecio odoratus

Variable groundsel
Senecio pinnatifolius

Kangaroo apple
Solanium aviulare

Dusty Miller
Spyridium parvifolium

Bower spinach
Tetragonia implexicoma

Grasstree
Xanthorrhea Australia

Regional Fungi

Winter is for wild weather and slippery walking on sections of the GOW, but it is also a time for marvellous, varied and colourful fungi. Some of the fungi are bold and chunky, others are delicate and tiny - just right for faeries at play. While some fungi may be edible, most are not, and can contain deadly toxins. We therefore encourage you to enjoy spotting them along the way, but avoid touching them. Identification can be difficult, even for experts, who examine the tops, the stems, the gills and the spores before making a positive identification. For that reason, we have chosen not to name the fungi in case we get it wrong, with potentially disastrous consequences, but have included photos of some we have found along the Walk to inspire you. The best sections of the GOW in which to find fungi are the wetter parts of the forests and rainforest gullies, in areas which are shaded from the sun and sheltered from the wind. You may get a close up view of them as you slip over on the wet clay and mud, as compensation for your efforts!

Useful Contacts

Great Ocean Road Coast and Parks Authority

The Great Ocean Road Coast and Park Authority (GORCPA) was established on 1st December 2020 as a Victorian Statutory Authority with a remit to 'manage, protect, rehabilitate and foster resilience of the natural, cultural and heritage values of coastal Crown land and marine waters along the Great Ocean Road.' Its main purpose is to protect and manage visitation to the Great Ocean Road and its Parks. It has a Board, which is made up of Traditional Owner representatives of the Wadawarrung and Eastern Maar, people with strong local community links, and various experts in conservation, marine protection, governance, tourism and planning. It is governed by its own Act of Parliament, The Great Ocean Road and Environs Protection Act 2020, and the coastal reserves it manages are being progressively transferred to it over the coming years. It also manages the public caravan parks from Torquay to Port Campbell, including Apollo Bay, Marengo and Princetown: www.greatoceanroadparks.com.au.

P.O. Box 53, Torquay VIC 3228   T 1300 736 533
info@greatoceanroadauthority.vic.gov.au
www.greatoceanroadauthority.vic.gov.au

Parks Victoria

Parks Victoria is responsible for the management of the National Parks along the GOW on behalf of the Great Ocean Road Parks and Coast Authority. Parks Victoria also provides visitor information about the Great Otways National Park and Port Campbell National Park, and hosts the official GOW campsite bookings. Please note that at the time of publication, the management arrangements between the GORCPA and Parks are being developed and are under transition, so details may change but it's unlikely to have a noticeable impact on walkers or visitors. Please check on the Parks Victoria website for any updates.

For all GOW camping information and bookings:
bookings.parks.vic.gov.au/great-ocean-walk.

For general information and current information on which parks and tracks are closed or having fire reduction burns: T 131 963, www.parks.vic.gov.au .

Emergency Victoria

For up-to-date information about current bushfire and flood warnings, and planned (controlled) burns: www.emergency.vic.gov.au

Tide times

Bureau of Meteorology: www.bom.gov.au/australia/tides/
Willy Weather: https://tides.willyweather.com.au/

Tourism Information Centres

An excellent one-stop shop website exists for visitors to the region: www.visitgreatoceanroad.org.au, but it is also worth going into the Visitor Information Centres in Apollo Bay, the Twelve Apostles and Port Campbell for their unbeatable local knowledge, helpful staff, free visitor guides and current maps.

Apollo Bay/Great Ocean Road Visitor Information Centre (start point of the GOW): 100 Great Ocean Road, Apollo Bay; T 131 963.

Twelve Apostles Visitor Information Kiosk (end point of the GOW): Cnr Booringa Road and Princetown Road, Twelve Apostles; T 131 963.

Port Campbell Visitor Information Centre (and shipwreck display): 26 Morris Street, Port Campbell; T 131 963.

Walking clubs

Bushwalking Victoria is the umbrella organization for walking clubs and individual walkers in Victoria, representing some 8000 walkers' interests, for those interested in joining organised groups. They can put you in touch with a suitable walking club who may organise walks along the GOW or sections of it. They also have an excellent website for members with downloadable map notes for walks and details of events across the State.

T 03 8846 4131
admin@bushwalkingvictoria.org.au
www.bushwalkingvictoria.org.au

Useful Contacts

Transportation options

Most GOW hikers travel via the Great Ocean Road by private car or tour company from Melbourne, so they can experience the stunning road itself as part of the adventure. However, on a one-way walk, if you are not camping, car shuttling (while possible) can be tricky and time-consuming due to the geography of the area.

Public Transport

While the GOW is not directly connected to rail, there are rail/bus options connecting from Melbourne (train) to Geelong and then to a bus service to Apollo Bay for the start of the walk. V/Line Trains run hourly from Melbourne to Geelong and are covered by the myki ticketing system (reservations are not required). On completion of the walk, you can take a bus from the Twelve Apostles to Warrnambool and then a direct country train back to Melbourne. Bus stopping points that intersect with the GOW are in italics:

Melbourne, Geelong, *Apollo Bay Information Centre, Marengo, Princetown Turn Off, Twelve Apostles Information Kiosk*, Loch Ard Gorge, Port Campbell Surf Club, London Bridge, Peterborough, Bay of Islands, Warrnambool.

Please note that the Walk is in a remote part of Victoria, and services may not run daily, depending on the season and day of the week. Check the Public Transport Victoria website for up-to-date timetables, as they change seasonally.

T 1800 800 007, www.ptv.vic.gov.au or download the PTV app

Private car shuttle / car parking

For those day walkers with two vehicles and extra time at the start and end of each day, the 'Build your own walk' table (pages 24-25) shows where you can leave your vehicles each day if doing a daily car shuttle: two cars drive to the finish of the day's walk. One is left there, while everyone goes in the first car back to the start. Critical point is not to lose your keys! For those camping/walking end-to-end who have come by car, it is possible to leave your vehicle (at your own risk) in the large car park at the Twelve Apostles Visitor Information Kiosk and catch the bus back to the walk start (parking fees may be payable). Alternatively, you can leave your car at the Princetown Recreation Reserve & Campgrounds and get the bus back to the start from the Princetown bus stop. There is a caretaker at the Campgrounds (T 0429 985 176 to make arrangements), so this may be relatively secure. If you park at Princetown, on the last day of the walk, you can drop your heavy packs off at your car on the way past before walking the final 6km to the Twelve Apostles, then either walk back, or catch the bus back to Princetown.

If you do leave your car anywhere, it is best to download a trip intention form from Victoria Police https://www.police.vic.gov.au/outdoor-and-bush-safety#trip-intentions-form and leave it visible on the dashboard of your vehicle so you don't inadvertently trigger a police search.

Commercial transport shuttle services

Regionally based shuttle services can be affordable for groups. They drop you off at the start of each walk and pick you up at the end of the day. They will provide services for independent groups as well as for tour groups, though you will need to book well in advance. While the services can be a little expensive, depending on the numbers in your group, it can literally save you hours of driving yourselves back and forth each day in your own car shuttles. Be aware that for some sections of the walk, and depending on where you are staying, it can be an hour or more to drive to your start/end point, and you will need to pre-agree times to meet them at designated spots at the end of the day. You will find the shuttle drivers to be full of excellent local knowledge and advice. In addition to the dedicated services below, some of the accommodation providers may also provide shuttle services for their guests (at an additional cost) if organised in advance, as indicated in the accommodation table.

Great Ocean Road Shuttle Bus service drops/picks up walkers along the GOW and elsewhere and is based centrally at Cape Otway. They can also organise airport pick up from Melbourne or Avalon to drop you at your Great Ocean Walk accommodation. T 03 5237 9278 or 0428 379 278; gorshuttle@bordernet.com.au.

Walk 91 will organise shuttle services as well as other GOW tour/support options. Based in Apollo Bay. T 03 5237 1189; www.walk91.com.au; info@walk91.com.au.

Ride With Us Great Ocean Walk Transport Service is part of the Timboon Taxi Service and can organise 24/7 drop off/pick ups, including to train stations and airports. T: 0438 407 777; www.ridewithus.com.au; hello@ridewithus.com.au.

Wildlife Tours Australia (based in Melbourne) offer a hop on/off option for people doing the GOW by prior arrangement. T 03 9393 1300; www.wildlifetours.com.au; info@wildlifetours.com.au.

Useful Contacts

Accommodation

Many walkers choose to complete the GOW as a series of day-walks, staying each night at accommodation locally rather than camping. There are a range of options available, from simple motels to farmstays and high-end lodges, caravan parks to glamping. With the increasing popularity of the Walk and its relative remoteness from towns, availability can be challenging, except at Apollo Bay and Port Campbell, where there is a great deal of choice. Many accommodation providers in the region also offer GOW Packages, including lunch packs, meals and transportation options. Have a good look at the regional map when booking — some walkers choose to book 2-3 different places to stay so they spend less time shuttling to and from the start/end of each day's walk, others prefer to base themselves centrally and settle in.

For accommodation in proximity to the GOW, ensure you ring and book well in advance, and check that your preferred accommodation will be open when you wish to walk — some are closed during the winter and the impact of Covid on tourism in the region has meant that some accommodation has either been temporarily or permanently closed. You will also be competing with tour operators who book for their own guests, so planning ahead is key. We have listed below contact details for some of the accommodation providers you will find along the Walk, though the list is not exhaustive and we have not included AirBnBs. Details of accommodation in Apollo Bay and Port Campbell can also be found at www.greatoceanroadaccommodation.directory. See Accommodation table on pages 130-131.

Self-guided and guided tour operators

If having it all organised for you, so you just turn up on the day to find all the arrangements are made, your lunch is packed ready for your daypack, accommodation booked, dinner ready for you on your return, along with a hot shower and clean sheets, there are a number of excellent and experienced tour operators who can offer either self-guided or guided walks. Some also offer supported camping options. Most of these are offered as 'pack-free', meaning that your main luggage is transported each day and you walk carrying just a day pack with your water, lunch, rain gear and camera etc. There are a range of choices, from 3-4 day 'highlights' for those with limited time, to the full end-to-end experience. Some offer high end glamourous experiences with massages, helicopter rides and gourmet meals; others will be more group lodges and shared facilities and everything in between. Maximum group sizes vary, though you can generally expect 8-16 people on public tours. If you are solo, it is worth asking if there is a single person supplement payable or not. There is something to meet everyone's needs.

We list some of the tour companies on page 129 to get you started, but we do not make recommendations nor receive payment for including them. Tour offerings can change so we strongly recommend you contact them directly for up-to-date details. Most companies now have flexible booking policies reflecting the uncertainty of travel since Covid, but it is advisable to check cancellation policies carefully.

Tour operator	Contact details	Tour products
All Trails Tours	www.alltrails.com.au alltrails@alltrails.com.au T 03 9802 4465	7 day, fully guided tours Local accommodation
Walk 91	www.walk91.com.au T 03 5237 1189 info@walk91.com.au	3-7 day self-guided, custom options Local accommodation Supported camping
AusWalk	www.auswalk.com.au T 1300 777 878 info@auswalk.com.au	4-8 days; guided/self-guided, custom options Local accommodation
Life's an Adventure	www.lifesanadventure.com.au T 02 9975 4553 walks@lifesanadventure.com.au	3 day pack-free highlights Local accommodation
Inspiration Outdoors	www.inspirationoutdoors.com.au T 08 6219 5164 walk@inspirationoutdoors.com.au	4 day highlights, 7 day end-to-end walk Local accommodation
OnlyLUXE Travel	www.onlyluxe.com.au T 02 8024 5937 info@onlyluxe.com.au	3-8 day guided options Lodge based
Wandering the World	www.wanderingtheworld.com.au T 0402 910 552 info@wanderingtheworld.com.au	4 days fully guided Local accommodation
Intrepid Travel	www.intrepidtravel.com T 1300 339 501 enquiries@intrepidtravel.com	4 days fully guided highlights Local accommodation
Australian Walking Company	www.auswalkingco.com.au T 1300 767 416 bookings@auswalkingco.com.au	4 days fully guided highlights Lodge based
Hike2Camp	www.hike2camp.com.au hike2campgow@gmail.com	4 day highlights, 6 days end-to-end Self-guided Supported camping
Hedonistic Hiking	www.hedonistichiking.com T 0428 198 918 info@hedonsitichiking.com	6 days, fully guided Local accommodation
Bang Fitness Adventures	www.bangfitness.com.au T 0400 207 303 info@bangfitness.com.au	4 days guided highlights Apollo Bay based accommodation

Accommodation

Accommodation	Email	Website
Marengo Area		
Marengo Family Caravan Park	marengo@greatoceanroadauthority.vic.gov.au	www.greatoceanroadparks.com.au
Cape Otway Area		
Bimbi Park	info@bimbipark.com.au	www.bimbipark.com.au
Shearwater Cottages	escape@shearwatercottages.com	www.shearwatercottages.com
Cape Otway Lightstation	keeper@lightstation.com	www.lightstation.com
Johanna Beach/Glenaire area		
The Boomerangs	bookings@theboomerangs.com	www.theboomerangs.com
Glenaire Cottages	info@glenairecottages.com	www.glenairecottages.com
Great Ocean Walk Retreat	bookings@greatoceanwalkretreat.com.au	www.greatoceanwalkretreat.com.au
Johanna River Farm & cottages	cottages@johanna.com.au	www.johanna.com.au
Johanna Seaside Cottages	info@johannaseaside.com.au	www.johannaseaside.com.au
Johanna Bluegum Holiday Cabins	johannabluegum@hotmail.com	www.johannabluegumholidaycabins.com.au
Wattle Hill/Moonlight Head area		
Alkina Lodge	info@alkinalodge.com.au	www.alkinalodge.com.au
Southern Anchorage Retreat	southernanchorage@bigpond.com	www.southernanchorage.com.au
By Moonlight	stay@bymoonlight.com.au	www.bymoonlight.com.au
Princetown area		
13th Apostle Backpackers	glennonpete@gmail.com	(no website at time of publication)
Macka's Farm	holidays@mackasfarm.com.au	www.mackasfarm.com.au
Pebble Point Glamping	contact@pebblepoint.com.au	www.pebblepoint.com.au
12 Apostles Motel and Country Retreat	booking@twelveapostles.com.au	www.twelveapostles.com.au
12 Apostles Cottages	12apostlescottages@gmail.com	www.12apostlescottages.com
Destination M	info@mnmrehab.com.au	www.mnmrehab.com.au

Address	Phone	Drop-off	Pick-up	Catering	Self-catering
15 Marengo Crescent, Marengo, VIC 3233	03 5237 6162	N	N	N	Y
90 Manna Gum Drive , Cape Otway, VIC 3233	03 5237 9246	Y	Y	Y	Y
760 Lighthouse Road, Cape Otway, VIC 3233	03 5237 9121	N	N	N	Y
Lighthouse Road, Cape Otway, VIC 3233	03 5237 9240	N	N	Enquire	Y
3815 Great Ocean Road, Johanna VIC 3238	0409 103 214	Enquire	Enquire	N	Y
3430 Great Ocean Road, Glenaire, Vic 3238	0433 911 584	N	N	N	Y
3229 Great Ocean Road, Glenaire, VIC 3238	0408 322 833	Y	Y	Y	Y
420 Blue Johanna Road, Johanna, Vic, 3238	03 52374219	N	N	Enquire	Y
395 Red Johanna Road, Johanna VIC 3238	03 5237 4242	Y	Y	Enquire	Y
705 Blue Johanna Road, Johanna, VIC 3228	0457 939 099	N	N	N	Y
35 Parkers Access Track, Wattle Hill, VIC 3237	03 8899 7426 or 0401 056 031	Enquire	Enquire	N	Y
50 Parkers Access Track, Wattle Hill, VIC 3237	0428 160 366	Enquire	Enquire	Y	Y
30 Parkers Access Track, Wattle Hill, VIC 3237	0427 581 575	N	N	N	Y
28 Old Post Office Road, Princetown, VIC 3269	0437 000 751	N	N	N	Y
2310 Pricetown Road, Princetown, VIC 3269	03 5598 8261	N	N	N	Y
20 Old Coach Road, Princetown, VIC 3269	03 5243 3579	N	N	N	Y
314 Booringa Road, Princetown, VIC 3269	03 5598 8277	N	N	Y	Y
771 Great Ocean Road, Princetown VIC 3269	0477 596 630	N	N	N	Y
6716 Great Ocean Road, Lower Gellibrand Vic 3237	0417 575 770	Enquire	Enquire	Y	Y

Further Reading

Books

Great Ocean Walk Information Guide & Official Map (6th Edition or later), Parks Victoria (2019) – a recommended companion to this guidebook. Comes in full map or spiral bound booklet form. 1:25,000 scale.

The Complete Guide to the Great Ocean Road (2009), Richard Everist

Best Walks of the Great Ocean Road (2016), Julie Mundy & Neil Fahey

The Field Guide to the Birds of Australia (2012), Graham Pizzey and Frank Knight

A Field Guide to Fungi of Australia, AM Young (2010) UNSW Press

Mystery at Moonlight Head: The Fiji Shipwreck Disaster of 1891 (2019), Alan McLean - available in regional shops, Port Campbell Visitor Centre, or from the author (0412 143660 or alanlmclean@bigpond.com)

'Our first class light': The role of Charles Joseph Latrobe in Building the Cape Otway Lighthouse' (2017), Tim Gatehouse in the Journal of the CJ Latrobe Society, vol 16, no. 3 (available online)

Xtreme Gourmet: High energy, lightweight recipes for the outdoor enthusiast (2015), Sonya Muhlsimmer, www.xtremegourmet.com

Useful websites, Facebook Groups and apps

www.parks.vic.gov.au/places-to-see/parks/great-otway-national-park/things-to-do/great-ocean-walk for general and up to date information about the walk, and details about planned Apps which will share stories of the Walk at various points as you walk along.

www.speakingoftheotways.net for detailed information on the Traditional Owners, flora, fauna and landscape of the Otways and the Great Ocean Road.

www.visitgreatoceanroad.org.au – Informative regional tourism website for the entire Great Ocean Road area.

www.conservationecologycentre.org – Cape Otway based conservation and research centre.

Field Guide to Victorian Fauna – informative and user-friendly free App via the iPhone App Store.

Further Reading

Fast Snake Identification (Australia Wide) - educative and friendly Facebook group run by professional herpetologists who will quickly identify any snake for you (by you uploading a photo with the date and location).

Victorian Hikers - friendly and helpful Facebook hikers group who are happy to answer questions as well as welcome uploads of your Victorian-based walk and experiences.

Australian Native Birds - helpful Facebook group for enthusiasts and amateurs who share their pictures and information about Australia native birds.

Australian Native Plant Enthusiasts Forum - Facebook group as above, focussed on plant life.

Australian and New Zealand Fungus Identification - Facebook page. Quite a serious and knowledgeable forum. You can upload photos of fungi (need photos of top, spores underneath and stems), along with a location and they will do their best to help you identify it.

Field Naturalists Club of Victoria - Facebook page. Plant and animal identification and interesting facts.

Hiking in Australia and New Zealand - active Facebook page with 50,000 members happy to share knowledge and ideas about bushwalking in general.

Index

A
accommodation, 10-11, 128, 130-131
Aire River, 65, 70

B
Bald Hill, 32
Bay of Islands Coastal Park, 105
Bay of Martyrs, 105
Blanket Bay, 45, 47, 50
Blanket Bay Massacre, 67
blue-ringed octopus, 112
Bowker Point, 81

C
camping, 10-13
Cape Otway Lightstation, 53, 58-59, 62
Cape Volney, 88
Castle Cove, 70
children, walking with, 7
cinnamon fungus, 74
Clifton Beach, 98
Crayfish Bay, 52

D
Decision points (mentioned in text),
- 1, 32
- 1A, 32
- 1B, 32
- 2, 32
- 2B, 33
- 3, 33
- 6, 44
- 6A, 45
- 6B, 45, 50
- 8A, 63
- 9, 72
- 9A, 73
- 9B, 73

Devils Kitchen, 91, 96, 97

E
Elliot Ridge, 42
Elliot River, 34
emergencies, 20
Emergency Victoria, 125
environment, care of, 18-19
Eric the Red, 50, 52, 55
Escarpment Lookout, 64

F
Fiji, 93, 97
fire and bushfires, 21, 109
food, 16
fur seals, 31

G
G.O.R. Coast & Parks Authority, 124
Gables Lookout, 91
Gadubanud, 2, 100
Gellibrand River, 97-98, 100
Gibson Steps, 99
Glenample Homestead, 98
Gog and Magog, 99
grading, walk, 6
grass trees, 74
guided walks, 8-9

J
Joanna, 74
Johanna Beach, 72, 78
Johanna Lookout, 78
Johanna River, 72, 74

K
koalas, 70

L
Latrobe Creek, 98
La Trobe, Charles, 82
leeches, 112
Loch Ard, 104
Loch Ard Gorge, 104
Logan Beach, 105
London Bridge collapse, 103, 105

M
Marengo Reefs, 35
Marie Gabrielle, 97
Milanesia Beach, 80
Milanesia Creek, 80
mobile coverage, 106
Moonlight Head Cemetary, 91, 93
Moonlight Head Lookout, 89
Mutton Bird Island, 105

O
Old Coach Road, 79

P
packing, 14-17
Parker Hill, 50-51
Parks Victoria, 124
Personal Locator Beacon, 106
Peterborough, 105
Phytophthora cinnamomi, 74
Point Franklin, 52
Point Lewis, 50
Point Roland, 98
poles, walking, 17
Port Campbell , 105
Port Campbell N.P. , 99, 102-104
Princetown, 98
Princetown Beach, 98

R
Rainbow Falls, 66
Rivernook Guesthouse, 97, 101
Ryans Den, 82, 88

S
Seal Point, 52
Sentinel Rock, 70
Shelly Beach, 34
snake bites, 110-111
Southern Bull Kelp, 35
Southern Right Whales, 38-39
Station Beach, 63
Storm Point, 32
swimming, 109

T
Three Creeks Beach, 33
Thunder Cave, 104
tides, 7, 108, 125
Tourism Information Centres, 125
Traditional Owners, 2-3
transport, 9-10, 126-129
trip intentions form, 106
Twelve Apostles, 99, 102-103

U
Upper Lookout, 73

W
walking clubs, 125
water, 17
weather, 3-4, 107
Wreck Beach, 91, 92, 96

Authors' Q&A

Who are you?

We are friends who met when our kids were at school together, and over the years discovered we shared a joy in bushwalking and open spaces. Deb happens to be a mountain goat and far fitter than Julie, who is more a 'forest bather/turtle-wanderer', but somehow we are quite sympatico in the walking stakes. Just as well, as this is now our third Victorian guidebook together. We both love being outside in wild spaces far more than inside. Julie hates leeches. Deb hates snakes. It balances out. Deb is a teacher and Julie an international aid worker, so this is definitely not our day job, though we both wish it was!

Did you actually walk the GOW yourself?

We walk all of our guidebook walks — often multiple times and from multiple angles and in different weather. We're not sure how you could write a guidebook without walking it yourself and why would you want to? It's the best part. We have individually and together walked the GOW a number of times over the decade and repeatedly in the lead up to the book, including all the detours and alternate routes, and at different tide times. We also speak to lots of locals, authorities, rangers, other walkers and operators to get their advice and insights, and to hear their stories.

Who is behind the scenes to help the guidebook happen?

It's a team effort for sure. Andrew Swaffer — our longstanding and encouraging editor at Woodslane Press, is the person who gets us over the line. Jenny Cowan is the cartographer and design genius, who interprets our squiggles and who makes it look lovely. Deb's husband, Andrew, is a map tragic and huge support of every shape and form. Accommodation is a bit of a family affair: Julie's lovely aunt and uncle in the Otways, John and Gail, and the always generous family of Deb's sis-in-law Alison in Lorne. A shout out too, to generous photographer friends who helped fill in some gaps: most particularly Greg Johns, a hiking fiasco in his own right, and Gail Hoiles, Nigel Hotston and Subhranil Das. Thank you also to Parks Victoria for their time and care of the GOW.

Photography credits

All photographs in this book have been taken by the authors, Debra Heyes and Julie Mundy, except as indicated below. Our sincere thanks to those who have so generously allowed us to use their beautiful photos to help illustrate our book.

Greg Johns (you legend - thank you!) pages vi, 17 (without poles), 26 (Station Beach), 41, 45 (ruins), 47 (sunrise), 58, 59, 60-61, 50 (view), 62 (koalas), 64, 65 (no shade), 69 (Johanna River), 73, 74, 75, 110, 112 (leech), 114 (swordglass butterfly, canary worm, blue tongue lizard, tiger snake), 115 (koala, black snail, swamp wallaby), 117 (wedge tailed eagle), 119 (hooded plover sign), 135.

Deb Sleigh p. 14 (pack contents)

Bob McPherson p. 39-40 (whales)

Sketch of *Eric the Red* on p.55 reproduced with thanks to Australian Maritime Collection purchased with USA Bicentennial Funds.

Painting on p. 82 by Eugene von Guerard, 1859-62, *Cape Otway* from the sketchbook, collection of the Dixson Library, State Library of NSW.

Alan McLean p. 93 (*Fiji* memorial)

Rivernook photos p. 101, Museums Victoria collection

Julian Finn p. 112 (octopus), Museums Victoria collection https://collections.museumsvictoria.com.au/species/8692

p. 113 (walkers on beach), Visit Victoria collection

Sharmaine Nockolds p 115 (platypus)

Michael J Fromholz p 115 (tiger quoll) with acknowledgment of the Conservation Ecology Centre Cape Otway, and Gunjan Pandey (potoroo), both Creative Commons by SA 4.0 https://creativecommons.org/licenses/by-sa/4.0 Wikimedia Commons.

David Paul p 115 (bush rat), Museums Victoria collection https://collections.museumsvictoria.com.au/species/8458

Gail Hoiles p. 116-7 (pardalote, singing honey eater, silvereye, grey fantail, gang gang cockatoo, yellow black tailed cockatoo, buff banded rail, cormorant, heron)

Nigel Hotston p. 116-7 (musk lorikeet, rainbow lorikeet, crimson rosella, willy wagtail, fairy wren, new Holland honeyeater, kookaburra, galah)

Subranhil Das p. 116-7 (pink robin, king parrot, sacred kingfisher, tawny frogmouth)

Benjamint444 p. 118 (hooded plovers, eggs), Creative Commons by-SA3.0 https://commons.wikimedia.org/w/index.php?curid=2829875

Lion Headland and Milanesia Beach

Woodslane Press

The Great Ocean Walk is just one of a growing series of outdoor guides from Sydney publishers Woodslane Press. To browse through other titles available from Woodslane Press, visit woodslanepress.com.au. If your local bookshop does not have stock of a Woodslane book, they can easily order it for you. In case of difficulty please contact our customer service team on 02 8445 2300 or info@woodslane.com.au.

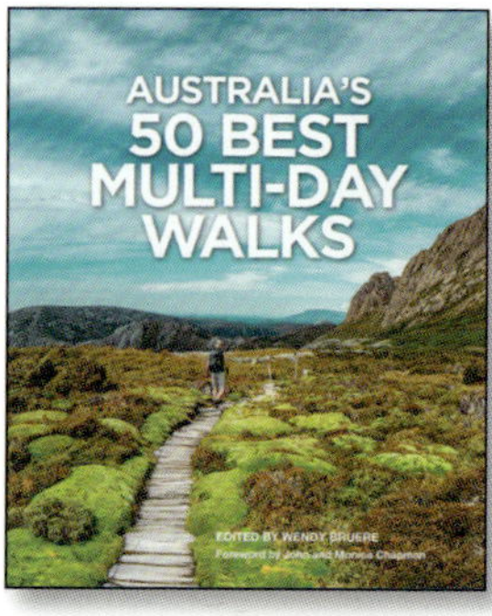

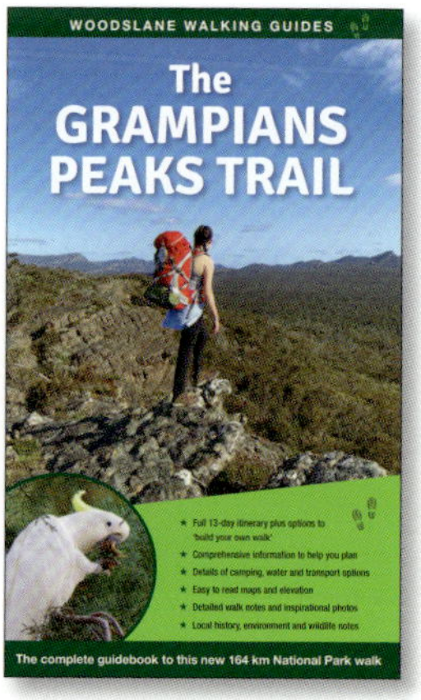

Titles include:

Best Walks of the Great Ocean Road

$24.99

ISBN: 9781922131829

Australian Geographic Great Ocean Road

$14.99

ISBN: 9781925868050

Australia's 50 Best Multi-day Walks

$34.99

ISBN: 9781922800619

The Grampians Peaks Trail

$29.99

ISBN: 9781922800091

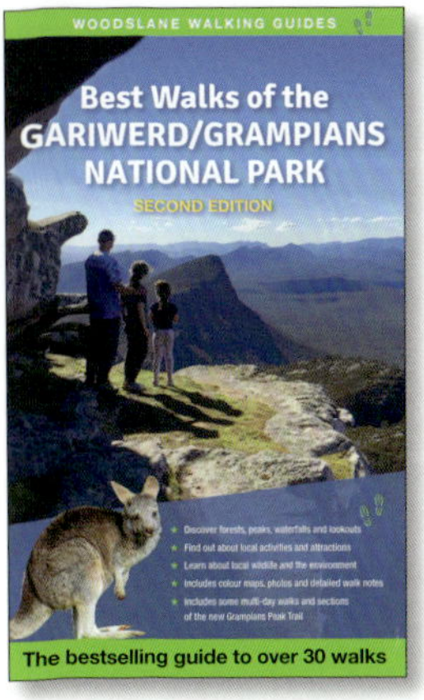

Best Walks of the Gariwerd/Grampians National Park

$29.99

ISBN: 9781925868951

Best Walks East of Melbourne

$32.99

ISBN: 9781922800725

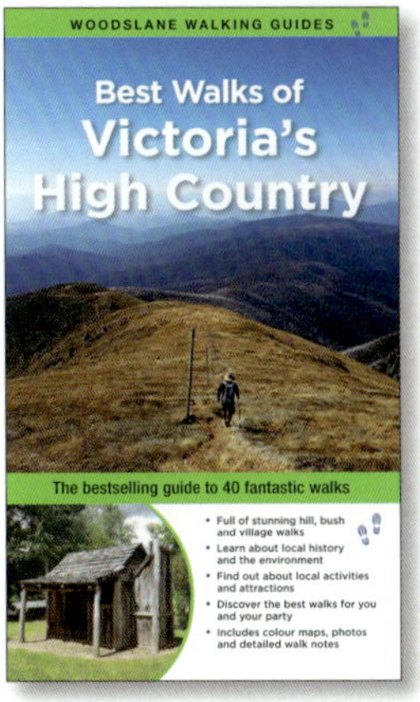

Best Walks of Victoria's High Country

$32.99

ISBN: 9781921874291

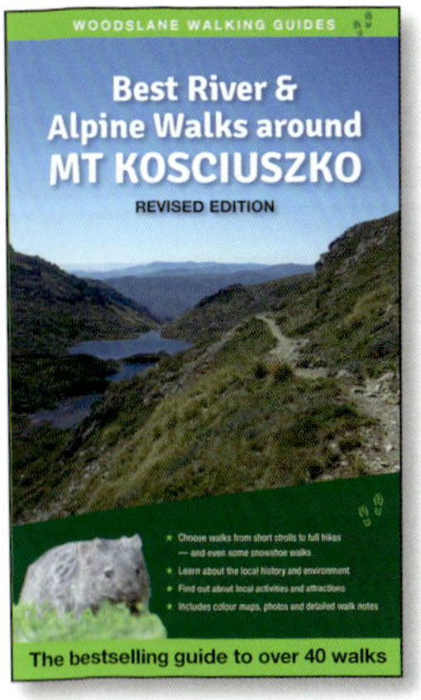

Best River & Alpine Walks around Mt Kosciuszko

$32.99

ISBN: 9781921606045

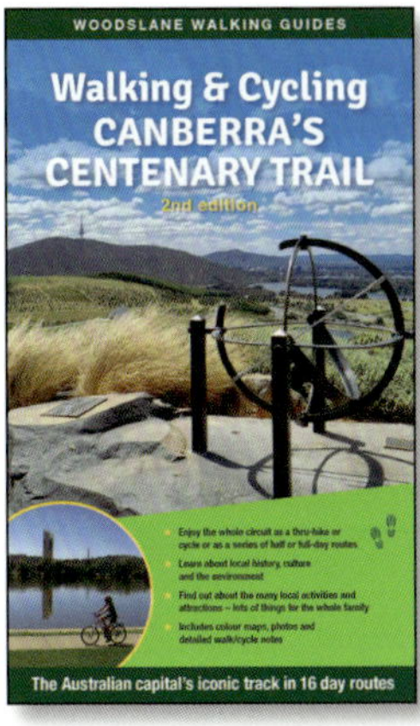

Walking & Cycling Canberra's Centenary Trail

$32.99

ISBN: 9781922800404

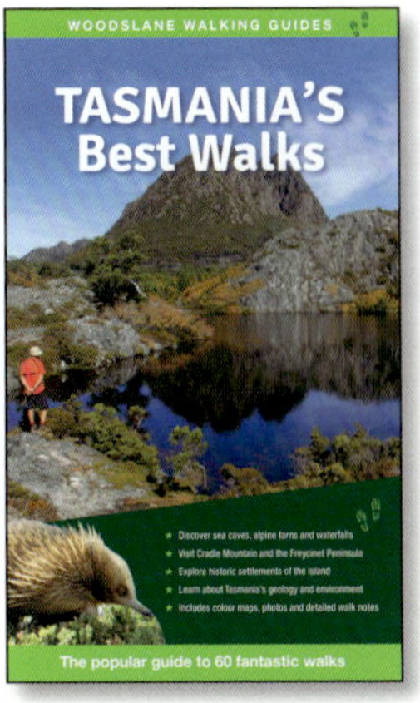

Tasmania's Best Walks

$34.99

ISBN: 9781925868890

Map Symbols & Legend